T0368086

A WALK TO LOVE

Wisdom He's Shared with Me

BAYLEE HEFLEY

WESTBOW
PRESS®
A DIVISION OF THOMAS NELSON
& ZONDERVAN

WestBow Press books may be ordered through booksellers or by contacting:

WestBow Press
A Division of Thomas Nelson & Zondervan
1663 Liberty Drive
Bloomington, IN 47403
www.westbowpress.com
844-714-3454

Interior Image Credit: Baylee J Hefley

Scripture taken from the New King James Version. Copyright © 1979, 1980, 1982 by Thomas Nelson, Inc. Used by permission. All rights reserved.

ISBN: 979-8-3850-3604-2 (sc)
ISBN: 979-8-3850-3605-9 (hc)
ISBN: 979-8-3850-3606-6 (e)

Library of Congress Control Number: 2024921595

Print information available on the last page.

WestBow Press rev. date: 12/04/2024

MY TESTIMONY

My story, like many others, is one of great falls and perfect grace. After being a Christian for seven years, I find myself in a posture of pride, vulnerable to the enemy's schemes. I'm nineteen years old, a naive Christian girl, believing men are generally good. The enemy was cunning; he knew my weaknesses and insecurities. I was not prepared for the temptations, the guilt, manipulation, and deception I would face through a very toxic relationship. Broken in sexual sin, I remember a moment of praying to the Lord, saying, "I'm ruined. I can't go through this heartbreak, so if I can't have You and this relationship, I choose him ..."

When Paul talks in Timothy (1:20) about handing people over to the devil so they learn not to blaspheme, this was my experience of being handed over, for the darkness that ensued in my life during this seven-month relationship was a darkness I had never felt before, and by the grace of God alone, I will never feel it again. Every day was nothing but a battle of hopelessness. I knew enough of the freedom of Jesus to know that I was living in a jail cell of my own sin. I knew I had chosen this, but I was drowning in the lies of Satan through this man. I was being told constantly that I was unlovable by anyone else. "What good, caring, self-respecting man would ever want washed-up goods like you?" I felt stuck, I felt hopeless, and I wanted to be dead. Death felt like the easiest way out of the mess I had dug myself into, which was why I planned it.

By the grace of Jesus, I couldn't carry it out. I couldn't stop thinking of my parents and what that would do to them. Two weeks later came some shocking news about the relationship I had been in for the last seven months. This discovery ended the relationship. As much as my heart was shattered and confused, there was also a sense of relief. I still didn't believe I had any worth, but maybe I could get away from this man. Maybe I could get closer to Jesus. I would never find a man who wanted me, but maybe I could at least be the toilet scrubber in heaven! Maybe I could at least find some forgiveness for walking away from the Lord. (Of course, my theology was all wrong in this thinking; we don't make it to heaven because we make the right decisions or because of any of our works, but that's a discussion for later on.) Little did I know, this was not the end but the beginning …

The beginning of Jesus's renewing. The beginning of realizing my worth in His eyes. The beginning of me experiencing and being able to proclaim Him to be the healer of the broken, the author of wholeness, the comforter of all.

I am now not only the bride of Christ but also the bride of an amazing man and blessed to be the mother to three sweet children, with another one on the way. My life has been completely redeemed.

This book has been seven years in the making. I pray it is the proclamation of all that I know Jesus to do and be, starting from Shortly after getting back from seven months in Mexico at a discipleship school. Mexico is where I found Jesus to be the absolute lover of my soul. I pray this book will be used for daily bites of remembering just how much He loves you.

FORGIVENESS

There is so much in the Bible about forgiveness; it seems to me that Jesus wants us to forgive one another.

But why? Because we are all rotten sinners. Not forgiving is a disease that poisons our attitude and outlook on life. Its first symptom is the belief that "I don't need to forgive because of what that person did to me"; its side effects are bitterness and hatred. The disease is subtle, slowly killing relationships and joy. I've heard it said harboring resentment is like drinking poison and expecting someone else to die; in reality, we're the ones slowly dying.

> Then Peter came to Him and said, "Lord, how often shall my brother sin against me, and I forgive him? Up to seven times?"
>
> Jesus said to him, "I do not say to you, up to seven times, but up to seventy times seven. Therefore the kingdom of heaven is like a certain king who wanted to settle accounts with his servants. And when he had begun to settle accounts, one was brought to him who owed him ten thousand talents. But as he was not able to pay, his master commanded that he be sold, with his wife and children and all that he had, and that payment be made. The servant therefore fell down before him, saying, 'Master, have patience with me, and I will pay you all.' Then the master of that servant was moved with compassion, released him, and forgave him the debt.

"But that servant went out and found one of his fellow servants who owed him a hundred denarii; and he laid hands on him and took *him* by the throat, saying, 'Pay me what you owe!'

... and his master was angry and delivered him to the torturers until he should pay all that was due to him." (Matthew 18:21–28, 34)

Without the forgiveness extended to me through Jesus, I would be condemned. Remembering the huge debt I've been forgiven of makes it so much easier to walk the path of forgiveness. Jesus was beaten beyond recognition, battered, mocked, ridiculed, spit on, and hung on a cross, all to *forgive* the very people performing these acts against Him—all to forgive me of my sins. If I can be forgiven, then I'd better be able to extend that forgiveness to others as well.

Forgiveness takes a daily process of choosing to lay down my pride, remembering I'm no better than anyone, and worse off than most without the forgiveness of my Lord and Savior, Jesus Christ, my only hope.

Do not say "I will do to him just as he has done to me: I will render to the man according to his work." (Proverbs 24:29)

Beloved, do not avenge yourselves, but *rather* give place to wrath; for it is written, "Vengeance *is* Mine, I will repay," says the Lord. (Romans 12:19)

PRAYER

Lord, help me forgive as I've been forgiven. You have given me so much grace, so I should all the more be understanding of the depravity and need of forgiveness in humanity because of our sinful, fallen state. You rescued me from hell; You set me free and gave me a clean slate. Help me give that same forgiveness to others.

CONTENTMENT

When I first got home to the States from Mexico, I had this overwhelming sense of contentment. I had a major realization, after being in a third world country for seven months, of how much we have and how much we take for granted. I was so content with just being home. It's amazing to me how quickly worries and distractions of this world can start to creep in, causing us to be unhappy even with the amazing blessings we do have and start to block our vision of what is truly important.

I learned a long time ago that I shouldn't make plans because life *never* turns out the way I think it will. I'm happy about this for so many reasons. Life would have been so much more boring if I was in charge of the course. But also, I've noticed that when I make plans for the future, I begin to just sit back in anticipation, waiting for the time to come for that plan to take place. I miss all the days, hours, and weeks in between. I miss all the chances to do what God has for me in this moment. We're never promised tomorrow; that's why He tells us to not worry about tomorrow, to live for today. Our society is one that drags through the workweek just to get to the weekend. What if we focused on living every day to the fullest with contentment? Wouldn't that be so much more satisfying? So much more meaningful?

> But Godliness with contentment is great gain. For we brought nothing into this world and it is certain we can carry nothing out. (1 Timothy 6:6–7)

PRAYER

Lord, give me a content heart. Knowing You alone can satisfy. You are our hearts' basic desire. You fill all the longing. Help me remember this anytime I feel the cares of this world try to steal my joy.

....

....

....

....

....

....

....

....

....

....

....

....

continue your personal prayer

STANDING

A little backstory. This was written directly after getting home from seven months in Mexico. I was struggling with restoring trust and relationships with family members who had been hurt by some bad choices I had made before I left.

Standing strong when you feel like you're standing alone is maybe one of the hardest things to experience. Especially when returning to a life and to people who used to know me, who know who I used to be—all my flaws and weaknesses before Jesus redeemed my life. The only way I will be able to stand is to remind myself I am not alone. I have a new identity, a new self-worth. I have been justified, cleansed, and set free.

When the attacks come, don't try to defend yourself; agree with your adversary. Remembering we don't fight against flesh and blood (Ephesians 6:12; paraphrased), say, "Yes, I've made mistakes. Yes, I am a sinner. No, I am no better than anyone else. But thankfully, I have a God in the business of setting sinners free. Thankfully, He has somehow offered me a gift, a new chance to be righteous, to be free from sin, guilt, and shame. I am rotten apart from Him. Apart from Him, there is no good in me. But He has made me new. I'm not who I was in the past." This world needs to see the broken people restored. They need to know there is hope. I'm here to tell you there is. If I can be free, then so can you. We who have the saving knowledge of what our Savior can do need to stop being selfish, like I have been, and need to be willing to tell a dying world, not just through words but through our lives, what they're missing. In return, we will be strengthened.

How shall they call on Him in whom they have not believed? And how shall they believe in Him of whom they have not heard? And how shall they hear without a preacher? And how shall they preach unless they are sent? It is written: "How beautiful are the feet of those who preach the gospel of peace, who bring glad tidings of good things!" (Romans 10:14)

PRAYER

Lord, help me stand. As a father holding his child's hand when he's learning to walk, so You hold me up; You are my support. Keep me in Your safety. Keep me in Your protection. Help me live this life for You.

continue your personal prayer

A HYPOCRITE, A LIAR

Jesus calls the Pharisees and scribes hypocrites in Matthew 23. It's easy for us to read this and say, "Yeah, what hypocrites. They were just prideful people, wanting to look better and more righteous than the rest." Then comes the conviction. The Pharisees were called hypocrites because they were doing works to be seen by others. When they would give, they would sound a bell on the street corners, letting everyone know they were giving. They wanted everyone to call them "teacher." They sat in the highest seats in the synagogue to let everyone know they were special and important.

When I was on a three-month mission trip to finish my discipleship training in Mexico, I battled with the same thing the Pharisees did. When we would go to churches to teach or travel around with our team, we were the missionaries. Although that was a big role that we should not have taken lightly, it was easy for me to get caught up in thinking I was a little more important than I really was.

You see, there is nothing special about me at all, except that Jesus lives inside me. Apart from Him, I'm just as messed up as anyone. When I was confronted with the issue of pride, I asked the Lord how to battle it. I was simply challenged to worship Him more in secret than I do in public. Speak to Him more in secret than I do in public. Give more of my life to Him in secret than I do in public. And if I haven't worshipped Him in secret the way I'm tempted to in public, it's a pretty good measure of hypocrisy in my life.

Sometimes writing can be something I have to check my heart on. When I write posts on my blog and on Facebook, at times I can begin to look at the likes and shares instead of saying to myself, "This is what God has put on my heart to write, and therefore the likes can't matter as much as obedience." When I write for likes, I can easily be confronted once again with that stinging word, *hypocrite*. If I'm writing for the applause of others, that is exactly what I am—a hypocrite. So once again, a little heart check for my motivation. It can't be for the applause of others, or I am no better than the Pharisees, and then I certainly have received my empty award in full.

> But you, when you pray, go into your room, and when you have shut your door, pray to your Father who *is* in the secret *place;* and your Father who sees in secret will reward you openly. (Matthew 6:6)

PRAYER

Lord, let my love be genuine toward You. Let temptation to fake holiness or be self-righteous be cut off. Let my heart be steadfastly, wholly Yours. Let the spirit of religious actions die. Let authentic relationship with You flourish in my soul.

....

....

....

....

....

....

....

continue your personal prayer

SEARCH FOR
HAPPINESS

It amazes me and fills me with sadness when I look around and see our world searching for happiness in places where all they will get is pain. I look back on my life and see at least one year when I was searching for the same thing in those same places. I see how it led to nothing but intense heartache. Although I know it wasn't God's plan for me to walk those paths and experience those things, He has now used those things for nothing but my good and His glory. In the time of repenting, I experienced the most comfort, healing forgiveness, restoration of my relationships with my family and friends, and the restoration of myself. It strengthened me, showing me my identity, my closest friend, my love, my Lord and Savior. The only one I need and the one who will always be there.

The only way I could ever understand healing and what Jesus could do in my life was by going through intense heartbreak, crying out for Him, and getting to the end of myself, my other people, and my resources, knowing He is all I have. Like I said, that wasn't His intention—it was the path I chose—but He will now use it to give me authority to tell others (maybe you who are reading this) that He is the healer of the broken. Give Him permission and watch Him work.

> Repent therefore and be converted, that your sins may be blotted out, so that times of refreshing may come from the presence of the Lord. (Acts 3:19)

PRAYER

Lord, I know You to be the healer, the mender of my brokenness. Thank You for being so kind. Thank You for Your comfort. Please come and transform my heart time and time again, making it more like Yours by the moment.

....

....

....

....

....

....

....

....

....

....

....

....

....

continue your personal prayer

AM I READY?

Yesterday, I had this question on repeat in my head. I have been studying the book of Matthew in my morning quiet times, and this morning I just happened to be in Matthew 24, which was the topic of a recent teaching in church. The basic resounding message is being ready for our Master coming. It really convicted me. Am I ready? It really would change the whole way I went throughout my day if I just remembered, *Oh, Jesus could be standing in front of me at any time, Is this the way I want to meet him?*

This chapter is so full of prophecy, warning us that we don't know the day or the hour but to be waiting and watching for Jesus to return. Wouldn't it change our focus and perspective if we kept this thought in the forefront of our minds? It would direct how and whom we talk to, what we say and why we say it. I definitely don't want to waste the precious time God has blessed me with. I want to use every second spreading His love and message. If only I could keep my focus 100 percent on Him.

> Watch therefore, for you do not know what hour your Lord is coming. But know this, that if the master of the house had known what hour the thief would come, he would have watched and not allowed his house to be broken into. Therefore you also be ready, for the Son of Man is coming at an hour you do not expect. (Matthew 24:42–44)

PRAYER

Lord, please be my focus. Let me remember You are the purpose of this life. I was created to worship You, for You to be on the forefront of my mind always.

....

....

....

....

....

....

....

....

....

....

....

....

....

....

continue your personal prayer

ATTACKS WILL COME

This morning, I woke up in a bad mood. All night, dreams woke me up, and memories of my past haunted me, so I couldn't go back to sleep. I started asking Jesus what He thought of me, and all those other things vanished. Darkness has no place with light.

Satan always wants to convince us that we are dirty, worthless sinners. I'm thankful I learned how to fight these thoughts he attacks me with. I simply agree. In humility, I have to agree I am such a sinner. I have made so many mistakes in my life, and the enemy of our souls will constantly remind us. It used to crush me, make me depressed, debilitate me, to where I believed I was so bad I couldn't be used by God. But now my strength is restored simply because I agree. I know apart from Jesus, I am a dirty, worthless sinner. But I thank Him every day that His blood covered those nasty things. When we feel ashamed, it's like throwing His sacrifice back in His face and saying it wasn't enough. We have to remember He did it for us, personally, and if I was the only person on earth, He would have done it only for me, only for you. So rest in His finished work, repent of the things you are ashamed of, accept His free gift that covers and makes you new, agree that you are dirty all alone, and find strength and comfort in the fact that He died for the sin of which you are ashamed.

Read Romans, chapter 6.

> Therefore, if anyone is in Christ, he is a new creation;
> old things have passed away; behold, all things have
> become new. (2 Corinthians 5:17)

PRAYER

Lord, let me always rest in your finished work on the cross. You paid it all for me. I've been made new through Your blood. Let me remember this when the attacks come.

....

....

....

....

....

....

....

....

....

....

....

....

....

continue your personal prayer

JUST DO IT

Since I got home from Mexico, I have been praying for God to open His next step for my life, not knowing if I am to start a job here or if He's planning to take me somewhere else in the world. I am of course learning to be content but still not wanting to start something here if it is not God's plan. While reading Matthew this morning, I noticed that Jesus many times asks the disciples to do things. These things make sense to us because we have the whole story, but to the disciples, some of those things made no sense at all.

> And He said "Go into the city to a certain man, say to him, 'The Teacher says, "My time is at hand; I will keep the Passover at your house with my disciples."'"
> (Matthew 26:18)

The disciples didn't even understand what "my time is at hand" meant, yet Jesus was asking them to say it to this random man. Sometimes God asks us to have faith and knock on doors, to say things that do not make sense. All we have to do is find and simply speak the things He tells us. But it takes a lot of faith to trust Him, and that's the point. He teaches us through these tests to simply trust Him and His plans. His plans are more exciting than we could ever have thought of for ourselves. So I'm learning. If He asks you to do something that seems out of this world, the best thing to do is be obedient in that moment.

PRAYER

Lord, let me be obedient whatever You ask, whenever You ask me. Let me have Your wisdom to make decisions that glorify You in this life. Teach me to be obedient.

....

....

....

....

....

....

....

....

....

....

....

....

....

....

continue your personal prayer

STRONG CHRISTIAN

Therefore let him who thinks he stands take heed lest he fall.
—1 Corinthians 10:12

There was once a time when I would have told you, "I am a strong Christian." I would never tell you that now. I am weak, I can do nothing in my own strength, and I am just a target for the enemy when I think I can. He will always attack, but if I'm fighting with my own strength, the battle is already lost.

In Matthew 26:31, Jesus tells the disciples once He dies, they will stumble. But Peter tells Him in verse 33, "Even if I have to die with You, I will not stumble." And all the disciples agree.

Peter feels like he is strong enough to stick with this thing. He's not going to stumble. He's got it under control.

Of course, later in the book, we see Peter deny his relationship with Jesus three times.

Jesus tells us, "Your spirit is willing, but your flesh is weak." When we say, "I'm strong. I can take on this world. I can stand up to it even if I have to die," we better be careful, because we are saying, "*I* can do this." When we say that we are fighting in *our* strength, we paint a bright red bull's-eye on our backs for the enemy of our souls. We should be saying, "Lord, I can do nothing! Please help me to stand, because only You can!" I don't know about you, but I don't want to be pretending I can fight this world and its darkness alone; it will chew me up and spit me out. But God, in us, is able to overcome it all.

PRAYER

Lord, I pray that I will stand in humility before You, that I will call on You and Your strength to fight for me, because I know You alone have the power.

....

....

....

....

....

....

....

....

....

....

....

....

....

continue your personal prayer

TRIALS IN LIFE

As a baby, if we never faced the trials of walking, we would never have learned to walk. If we never faced the trials of eating food, we'd still be drinking from a bottle. If we never faced the trial of potty training … well, you get the point.

Our walk with Jesus is a lot like this. I've asked many times in life, "Why am I facing this again?" Well, remember being a baby learning to walk? Remember how much you cried and how many times you fell and had to get back up? It's the same with learning to walk this life with Jesus. But if we just stay down, keep crawling, and never stand up, we will never run, because we haven't even conquered walking. Sometimes, as people who have been walking for a long time, we forget the learning process we went through as babies. But our walk with Jesus is the same; we will walk, we will fall, we will get back up and do it again. Otherwise, we will never grow. But if we keep practicing, eventually, we will run! I am faced with this challenge this morning. "In times when you face a trial, remember you are learning. Keep practicing and keep growing through this, or you will be stunted and never mature." The faster we learn the next skill, the faster we will develop in our relationship and become mature Christians.

> And not only that, but we also glory in tribulations, knowing that tribulation produces perseverance; and perseverance, character; and character, hope. Now hope does not disappoint, because the love of God has been poured out in our hearts by the Holy Spirit who was given to us. (Romans 5:3–5)

PRAYER

Lord, help me embrace the trials, knowing that trials are necessary to build in me strength and character. Let Your joy be my strength in every circumstance.

....

....

....

....

....

....

....

....

....

....

....

....

continue your personal prayer

OH, HUMILITY

The fear of the Lord is the instruction of
wisdom, and before honor is humility.
—Proverbs 15:33

Humility is not a fun thing to learn. In order to learn humility, you must go through humiliation. God has used humiliation in my life to remind me that I am not the special one. Anytime I start to think more highly than I ought to think of myself, humiliation comes to bring me down a notch or two. Jesus has used humiliation to remind me that I cannot do anything good on my own. Without His guidance, I make a mess of my life. Humiliation can be a tool from the Lord to train us spiritually, but humiliation can also come from the wounds left by sin. Sometimes you think a wound is all healed up, and then it breaks open again, revealing more of the infection you have to clean out, re-doctor, and re-bandage. The more a wound breaks open, the bigger the scar is, but if infection is present, opening it up again is the only way it can heal. Scars keep us humble, because they are a reminder of the wound sin caused and a reminder of our failures without God's guidance. We need to revere our scars, respect the pain, and let it always be a reminder to us to not go back to that place, to always bring us back to the only one who can make us stand, the only one who can protect us, the only one able to heal—Jesus, our Lord.

PRAYER

Lord, let humility be a stamp on my life. Let me always walk humbly, knowing that You alone deserve any glory.

JESUS'S POWER

I've read the book of Matthew a few times. I feel like if I'm not careful, the accounts of Jesus can lose their power. I read chapter 27 today. It is about the torture that Jesus went through. He was silent as they hurled insults and false accusations, silent as they mocked Him and beat Him, silent as they drove nails through His hands and feet. He was innocent. Was He weak or powerless? Could He not do anything against them? No. And yet we see the first time He speaks during the crucifixion, Mark's Gospel tells us He asks for His Father to forgive them (to forgive us). My sin nailed him to that cross. This story should make such a bigger impact on me each and every time I read it. When I'm dealing with hard things in my life, when I'm tempted to yell and get angry that things aren't going my way, I should remember how my Savior, innocent, all powerful, holy Lamb of God, humbly took my rightful place and became the sacrifice for me, because He loves me that much. I grew up on this message. But until I actually put myself in His shoes, it doesn't have any effect. I ask myself how it would feel to be left by everyone who says they love you, be mocked before a counsel of people making false accusations, be spit on, beaten and crucified, all while silently doing it for the people who are causing you so much pain.

Lord, this is the type of character I want to have, but I don't want to go through the trials. The trials are what produces character. Embrace the trials, remembering He went through a lot more than me, by me (because it was our sin that put Him on that cross), and for me, because He loves me and because He loves you. Maybe viewing life through this lens, we can begin to see our problems as the light and momentary (2 Corinthians 4:17) afflictions that they are in the grand scheme of eternity in heaven.

> Then the soldiers of the governor took Jesus into the Praetorium and gathered the whole garrison around Him. And they stripped Him and put a scarlet robe on Him. When they had twisted a crown of thorns, they put it on His head, and a reed in His right hand. And they bowed the knee before Him and mocked Him, saying, "Hail, King of the Jews!" Then they spat on Him, and took the reed and struck Him on the head. And when they had mocked Him, they took the robe off Him, put His own clothes on Him, and led Him away to be crucified. (Matthew 27:27–31)

PRAYER

Lord, let me always be in awe of Your power. Let me remember just how meek and humble You were when You walked this earth. Let me do my best to imitate Your character.

....

....

....

....

....

....

continue your personal prayer

A WAR WE CAN'T SEE

We cannot relax; we are in a war—a war we can't see.

> For we do not wrestle against flesh and blood, but against principalities, against powers, against the rulers of the darkness of this age, against spiritual hosts of wickedness in the heavenly places. (Ephesians 6:12)

We face a war every day. Sometimes it can feel like we're fighting other people, but the real war is against our own flesh. Think about it. Getting defensive and fighting with others is a choice we make in our minds. It takes at least two people to fight; if one of those people won't fight, then there is no fight. Most of the time, fights happen because of poor communication, a misunderstanding. But in our minds, we feel entitled to be upset, so we get defensive; the people we seem to be fighting are also wrestling with their own minds.

Satan loves division. He likes to sprinkle in lies that they will easily believe or shame that cuts deep to take this fight to the next level. He can torture us with this rabbit trail of past failures until we lash out at others, causing them to clap back. You see, a lot of times, the enemy of our souls takes our feelings, thoughts, and insecurities and uses them against us to create a fake scenario worth fighting other people. During the earliest years of marriage, I can't count the number of times I had been in an argument with my dear husband and said to him, "So you think I'm … (fill in the blank)," only for him to say, "What? You're putting words in my mouth; I didn't say that." But someone did! The enemy of our souls is where those thoughts come from, and if we're not quick to recognize it, our relationships can suffer. When you come across a defensive person, remember they're not fighting you; they're wrestling with themselves, and in turn, they lash out at you. Maybe keeping this in mind will help us be more like Jesus, with grace and patience toward other people, remembering we are all fighting a battle. We've all got the same enemy. Have grace with one another.

PRAYER

Lord, please fight for me. Please be my shield and protection in this life. Let me rely on You. Let me remain in Your presence.

....

....

....

....

....

....

....

....

....

continue your personal prayer

FICKLE FAME

I find it interesting that in the beginning of Mark's Gospel, he tells us all about how popular Jesus is; the demons know His name, people are coming at Him from all directions, and He can't be in a solitary place without someone looking for Him. But starting the book of Mark after just finishing Matthew really shows me something. Those people who love Jesus so much in the beginning will soon be the same ones yelling, "Crucify Him!" Why? Well, the only accusation they brought against Jesus was that "He tells the truth."

We don't have to look too far into our society to realize that we are not a people that like truth either. And if you're a person talking about controversial things (a.k.a. truths of the Bible), it may not be too long before someone disagrees with you as well. Jesus says, "If they hated me, how much more they will hate you." If we are truly serving Jesus with our lives, we can be sure we will have some enemies. We have to be careful we're not putting our identity into what people say of us, because the same people who are singing our praises now could be yelling, "Crucify him!" tomorrow. We're not perfect like Jesus was, and the majority of people aren't quick to forgive; one wrong move or misspoken word could mean cancellation in this day. They hated and crucified Jesus. What does that mean for us? Well, it can be scary if we're looking to please people. We must put our identity in Jesus instead, obeying what He says and looking forward to the prize set before us. We must not put any weight on building our kingdom here on earth but rather on storing up those treasures where moth and rust do not destroy (Matthew 6:19–24).

"If the world hates you, you know that it hated Me before it hated you. If you were of the world, the world would love its own. Yet because you are not of the world, but I chose you out of the world, therefore the world hates you. Remember the word that I said to you, 'A servant is not greater than his master.' If they persecuted Me, they will also persecute you. If they kept My word, they will keep yours also. But all these things they will do to you for My name's sake, because they do not know Him who sent Me." (John 15:18–21)

PRAYER

Lord, let me not seek the glory of this life. Let me be focused on Your kingdom and storing up treasures there. Every bit of this life is fickle, but it gives us the ability to have treasures in eternity. Help me to remember this truth.

....

....

....

....

....

....

....

continue your personal prayer

THE MUNDANE

It's unbelievable how fast I can fall into a routine. I do the same thing every day: wake up, get coffee, read the Bible, write a prayer, work out, go to work, come home, eat dinner, go to sleep, to do it all over again tomorrow. Somethings can become ritual, not that I consciously make it so; things just become routine and mundane. I was reminded this morning when God asked me, "Are you doing this time *for* Me or *with* Me?" This question really hit me. God wants our hearts, not our services. Reading the Bible means nothing to Him if we're doing it out of routine or habit. He wants to spend time with us, pouring His heart and love into us. It's so easy to read our couple chapters to be good little Christians and then get on with our lives. But it is completely worthless if He's not a part of it. This is a relationship, not a routine. What if you sat down with a friend every day and said, "I have thirty minutes. I'll tell you what I want you to do for me, and I'll read your biography, but you don't get to say anything because I'm kind of running late." Well, you wouldn't have a very good relationship with that friend; they probably wouldn't stick around very long. But this is how I treat my Lord and Savior sometimes. Jesus deserves our time, and how incredible is it that even though I do treat Him like this, He still wants a relationship with me.

> My beloved spoke, and said to me: Rise up, my love,
> my fair one, and come away. (Song of Solomon 2:10)

PRAYER

Lord, it's a relationship with me that You want. Help me to not fall into a religious mindset, thinking that reading and praying makes me holy. Reading and praying does nothing unless You are there, unless I am communicating with You.

....

....

....

....

....

....

....

....

....

....

....

....

continue your personal prayer

WHAT SEED
ARE YOU?

Chapter 4 of Mark is one of my favorite parables that Jesus speaks. Jesus met the people where they were on a level they could understand. In this case, in agriculture.

There are so many different life application avenues we can take with this text, but I'd like to highlight just one today. I'm sure we'll be revisiting this analogy again.

The sower—which should be us—is just responsible for scattering the seed, not being careful of where it lands, not placing it strategically to make sure it will produce. No. Scatter the seed. It says some seed fell on rocks, some in weeds, and some in good soil, but in order for it to grow, it had to be scattered. Which means everywhere we go, we walk, talk, and live in such a way that shows others who our God is. I don't know about you, but there are times and seasons when I don't feel I'm doing this well. It's a big order to fill, but that's what we're called to. How do we accomplish this? In Mark, chapter 4, verse 34b, it says, "And when they were alone, He explained all things to His disciples."

That is the key, to get alone with Jesus, because with alone time comes relationship, with relationship comes intimacy, and with intimacy comes understanding. Jesus didn't explain everything to everyone. He only explained to those who had a desire to be in deep relationship with Him, those who walked to the quiet place with Him. This is where I want to be, and this is the only place we can be truly effective in scattering the seed everywhere we go.

PRAYER

Lord, let my love and relationship with You be intimate. Let me seek the quiet time with You, for it's there that you produce understanding.

....

....

....

....

....

....

....

....

....

....

....

....

....

....

continue your personal prayer

ONLY BELIEVE

Chapter 5 of Mark hit me hard this morning. Our Jesus is just so amazing.

While traveling to the house of a synagogue ruler whose daughter was dying, Jesus stopped to acknowledge a woman who had been healed by the faith of just simply touching His clothes. She was already healed. He could have just kept going. He did have another pretty important thing to do. But He stopped to talk to this woman. He told her in verse 34, "Daughter, your faith has made you well. Go in peace and be healed of your affliction."

He says this same thing to you and me! We have to accept the gift of healing! What if she sat back down and didn't do anything different? Everyone who knew her would still believe she was that same woman dealing with the same disease. When we've been healed, we need to *go* in peace and believe in His promises in a way that shows others the hope that lives within us. We must live accepting that He has made us clean. He has healed us, and we need to acknowledge His change in our lives.

Now that's all fine and dandy, but fast-forward a few minutes and see that the little girl Jesus was on His way to save is dead. No doubt the ruler is saying, at least to himself, "If Jesus had just kept moving, my daughter would have been saved. Why did He heal this woman and not my daughter?" But Jesus says, "Do not be afraid: only believe." Jesus walks us through these times of despair so He can show His true power. If the girl hadn't died, Jesus wouldn't be able to raise her from the dead. But He does. He raises her from the dead. He brings glory to Himself through this miracle.

Maybe today, like me, you relate to the woman healed needing to go in peace and walk in that healing and forgiveness, or maybe you're the one who's overcome with grief, and you have no idea what Jesus was doing, why He was "wasting" time. Remember that no matter what, He is always faithful. Bring Him your situation today. Surrender it and watch Him comfort your heart.

"Do not be afraid: only believe." (Mark 5:36)

PRAYER

Lord, I know You are sovereign over everything, and I know that You will use everything for my good and Your glory. Right now, I'm hurting, but You are near to the brokenhearted. Please comfort my soul. Please heal my heart.

....

....

....

....

....

....

....

....

continue your personal prayer

THE NURSE

Jesus faced a lot of persecution in chapter 6 of Mark. I started thinking about how to handle persecution in my life.

Let's think of this life as a hospital. Everyone who is living apart from knowing their creator represents a sick or injured person; after all, He is called the Great Physician. So, at times when I am not a person in need of the hospital services (I am in need of them a lot), I get the pleasure of being His nurse. I just assist in preparing hearts for surgery by the greatest physician.

I've never been a nurse, but I have seen some mean people when they are in pain. They lash out at the nurses because of this pain. Now if the nurses looked at the patients and said, "Fine. Take care of yourself. I'm leaving," the patient would never be prepped for the doctor to do what he needs to do. If we are cleaning wounds, if we are touching on the places in people's lives where they have been hurt, they're going to lash out. As a good nurse, it's important that we remember they are not lashing out at us; they are lashing out at the pain. I might be the cause of the pain due to the procedure that needs to be performed. Cleaning out infections is very painful, but the pain is necessary for healing. I've been in the metaphorical surgery room being operated on. I've had metaphorical nurses prepping me for God's work to be done on my heart. I don't believe I was always kind to those individuals, but I sure thank God for them now. Without them, I'd still be walking around with a gaping infection plaguing my life.

Blessed are those who are persecuted for righteousness sake, For theirs is the kingdom of heaven. (Matthew 5:10)

PRAYER

Lord, let me be a compassionate nurse. Let me be Your hands and feet to those around me. Thank You for the opportunity to be used in other people's lives for healing. I pray for courage and strength.

....

....

....

....

....

....

....

....

....

....

....

continue your personal prayer

POLITICALLY
CORRECT?

While reading Mark this morning, I came to the realization that Jesus wasn't worried about being politically correct. In 7:25, we see a woman come to Jesus, asking Him to heal her daughter from demon possession. His answer is "Let the children be filled first, for it is not good to take the children's bread and throw it to the little dogs."

When I first read this, I thought, *How could Jesus be so harsh? He's Jesus. Isn't He supposed to be loving? He's literally calling her a dog.* But the more I thought about it, the more I realized this is the most loving thing Jesus could have said and done to her. What if He just said, "I'm tired. I just want to be alone, so go your way. Your daughter is healed"? She would have gotten what she wanted but wouldn't know what she needed. Instead, He's saying, "You're not My child. You first need to realize your true need is for Me, before I will heal your situation." And she does realize her need because she says, "I know I'm just a little dog. I know You can do much more amazing things for Your children. I know I'm not worthy, but I just want the crumbs of what I know You're able to do." And it says her faith in Him is what healed her daughter. Maybe you feel Jesus is being difficult or unloving with you. But look for the understanding He is trying to use the struggle to uncover. Because, like this woman, when you realize what He's trying to teach you, the struggle is all worth it.

Then He said to her, "For this saying go your way; the demon has gone out of your daughter." And when she had come to her house, she found the demon gone out, and her daughter lying on the bed. (Mark 7:29–30)

PRAYER

Lord, give me wisdom and help me know that every struggle I face in this life is for my good and Your glory.

....

....

....

....

....

....

....

....

....

....

....

continue your personal prayer

BUT HOW

I had to laugh when I started Mark, chapter 8, this morning. Jesus says, "Let's feed these four thousand people." The disciples look at him and say, "How?"

This is truly the point when I'm amazed Jesus's humanity doesn't kick in and say, "The same way I fed them just two chapters before! Only this time, we have more food and fewer people!" This is obviously not what he says. He just says, "How many loaves do we have?"

Seven.

"Okay, sit the people down." We will do this *again*. Maybe this time you'll actually get it, guys!

He feeds them all and once again the disciples pick up full baskets of food.

This doesn't really have much of an effect on them; they completely miss it again, because they get in the boat, and Jesus speaks to them about pride using a yeast analogy, and they think He's criticizing them for not bringing bread.

He's like, "Guys, get off the bread subject. Don't you realize what I did twice right before your eyes? I don't need much; I can make it a lot. I'm not talking about bread."

I find I'm the same way most of the time! I see God provide something from nothing. He provides above and beyond for me. Then the next second, I doubt He will this time. I ask the same silly question, "How?"

I thank Him for being so patient with me.

PRAYER

Lord, I thank You so much for Your patience with me. So often, I'm lost in my understanding of life, but You remind me again and again You are in control. Please use my life for Your glory!

....

....

....

....

....

....

....

....

....

....

....

....

....

continue your personal prayer

CRIED OUT ALL
THE LOUDER

Now they came to Jericho. As He went out of Jericho with
His disciples and a great multitude, blind Bartimaeus, the
son of Timaeus, sat by the road begging. And when he
heard that it was Jesus of Nazareth, he began to cry out
and say, "Jesus, Son of David, have mercy on me!"
Then many warned him to be quiet; but he cried out
all the more, "Son of David, have mercy on me!"
So Jesus stood still and commanded him to be called.
Then they called the blind man, saying to him,
"Be of good cheer. Rise, He is calling you."
And throwing aside his garment, he rose and came to Jesus.
So Jesus answered and said to him, "What
do you want Me to do for you?"
The blind man said to Him, "Rabboni,
that I may receive my sight."
Then Jesus said to him, "Go your way; your faith
has made you well." And immediately he received
his sight and followed Jesus on the road.
—Mark 10:47–52

This little piece of Mark 10 really spoke to me.
As soon as this man heard the name *Jesus*, he knew there was
power. He knew that this man could heal him. He cried out for him.
When people told him to be quiet, he cried out all the louder. When
Jesus says, "Come here," it says he throws away his clothes.

There is brokenness in me. I only see it more clearly the longer I walk with Jesus. He is the only one who can heal me. Am I crying out for Jesus? I know His power, and I know what He can do. Am I crying out with all I have for Him to do His work in my heart, not caring who is around, who is telling me to be quiet? Am I casting away everything to come to Him when He calls me? Close to Him is the only place I will receive sight.

PRAYER

Lord, I pray You would heal the brokenness in my life. Give me sight. Let me realize my depravity and my utter need for You! Help me cry out all the louder for You!

....

....

....

....

....

....

....

....

....

....

continue your personal prayer

WILLINGLY
IGNORANT

There's ignorance, and then there is being willingly ignorant. Being willingly ignorant is just simple disobedience disguised as being uneducated.

Jesus is asked a question, designed to trap Him, in Mark 11:28, "By what authority are you doing these things? And who gave you this authority to do these things?"

Personally, if I was Jesus, I'd be irritated by now. "How many times do I have to tell you? How many miracles do I have to perform for you to believe in me?"

Jesus knew they were trying to catch Him with any words they could use against Him. He replies to this question with one of His own.

> But Jesus answered and said to them, "I also will ask you one question; then answer Me, and I will tell you by what authority I do these things: The baptism of John—was it from heaven or from men? Answer Me." (v. 29–30)

Jesus is never in a hurry to defend Himself; He is never quick to give answers.

> And they reasoned among themselves, saying, "If we say, 'From heaven,' He will say, 'Why then did you not believe him?' But if we say, 'From men'"—they

feared the people, for all counted John to have been a prophet indeed. So they answered and said to Jesus, "We do not know." (v. 31–33)

When I see this in my head, I picture it as that game show on TV, *Family Feud*. Jesus asks them a question. They all huddle together. "We could say this, but then he'll have us trapped. But if we say that, then *they* won't like it. We'll just have to go with the safe answer." Then they turn to Jesus. "Okay, we've got it. Final answer, Jesus. We're locking it in. We don't know."

We see here they are not worried about the truth. They didn't care to really search into their hearts to know truth; they just wanted a reason to kill Him. They had no answer that would accomplish their agenda, so they chose to act ignorant.

I did this when I was little with my parents. They'd ask a question that may or may not have gotten me into trouble, so instead of answering with truth, I would answer with the only safe answer, "I don't know." The reality is I did know, but I chose to look ignorant rather than guilty. I have to be diligent not to do this when I'm asked a question by God. Sometimes He touches on areas I don't want to be truthful with; even if it's honesty with myself, I'd rather choose ignorance. But He tells us in proverbs,

> The lips of the righteous feed many. But fools die for lack of wisdom. (Proverbs 10:21)

There is ignorance, and then there is choosing to be ignorant. We must choose to be wise and truthful, whether it hurts our pride and agenda or not.

And Jesus answered and said to them, "Neither will I tell you by what authority I do these things."

Jesus doesn't give them an answer because He knows they don't sincerely want an answer. Let us be wise in answering the world's questions. Let us be quick and shrewd when listening, and let us be slow to defend ourselves.

BAYLEE HEFLEY

PRAYER

Lord, please fill me with Your Holy Spirit. Let me be wise as a serpent but innocent as a dove. Let me conduct myself with Your character in every way.

....

....

....

....

....

....

....

....

....

....

....

....

continue your personal prayer

- 68 -

HOW CAN IT BE?

Remembering what God has brought me out of is always a good way to be humbled. I'm nothing without Him. I've tried living without Him. I just found emptiness among other life afflictions, going through the motions of every day without much hope. I'm so thankful to have been brought out of that, but oh how afraid I am of walking away from my Lord again.

Even though I know without a doubt that I am nothing without Jesus, the flesh within me doesn't want to believe that. How easy it is for pride to creep in and make me think I can be strong in myself. Anytime the enemy can get me to take my eyes off of Jesus and put any sort of reliance on my own strength, I can be certain the battle is already lost. In Mark 8:15, Jesus refers to pride as yeast; yeast puffs things up, and "a little leaven, leaven's the whole lump" (1 Corinthians 5:9). If I'm not careful to keep pride out of my life, the *yeast* will infiltrate every part of it, and I will be rendered ineffective in living this life in Jesus's likeness. I have been saved, but escaping the fire of hell is not merely the point. God desires for us to live life with Him to the fullest! With every day more exciting and fruitful than the last. When we fully trust in Him, when we do what He tells us, there is nothing that could be more fulfilling in this life. He has a plan for all of our lives, and it's simply better than ours.

> Therefore we also, since we are surrounded by so great
> a cloud of witnesses, let us lay aside every weight, and
> the sin which so easily ensnares us, and let us run
> with endurance the race that is set before us, looking
> unto Jesus, the author and finisher of our faith, who

for the joy that was set before Him endured the cross, despising the shame, and has sat down at the right hand of the throne of God. (Hebrews 12:1–2)

He holds your future. He holds you. You do not need to fear. Love Him, and everything else will fall into place.

PRAYER

Lord, Let my heart rest in Your faithfulness and power. Let me not be afraid of tomorrow, knowing You are already there. You have the best plan. Let me remain in Your will.

....

....

....

....

....

....

....

....

....

....

continue your personal prayer

WORSE BEFORE
BETTER

When some of Jesus's disciples ask what the signs of the end-times will be, He answers in 13:7–8 by saying, "But when you hear of wars and rumors of wars, do not be troubled; for such things must happen, but the end is not yet. For nation will rise against nation, and kingdom against kingdom. And there will be earthquakes in various places, and there will be famines and troubles. These are the beginnings of sorrows."

We see many of these *signs* all around us right now. We have many rumors of wars, natural disasters, troubles, and unrest in various places. If our eyes aren't on heaven, these things can make us weary. Jesus says none of this should make us nervous, for He is sovereign over it all. When we watch the news and things seem to be falling apart, we can read this passage and know, according to Jesus Himself, things are actually falling into place exactly the way He said they would. Instead of being fearful, this should make us excited, for we know Jesus is coming back soon, but it should also move us to share this news with the people who don't know Him. This is where it can get a bit scary, especially as we keep reading. If the wars and rumors of war are true, then the persecution He talks about in the next few verses is also coming.

> "But watch out for yourselves, for they will deliver
> you up to councils, and you will be beaten in the
> synagogues. You will be brought before rulers and
> kings for My sake, for a testimony to them. And

the gospel must first be preached to all the nations. But when they arrest you and deliver you up, do not worry beforehand, or premeditate what you will speak. But whatever is given you in that hour, speak that; for it is not you who speak, but the Holy Spirit. Now brother will betray brother to death, and a father his child; and children will rise up against parents and cause them to be put to death. And you will be hated by all for My name's sake. But he who endures to the end shall be saved." (Mark 13:9–13)

Jesus tells them, "These persecutions will give Me through you the opportunity to speak and witness to people you wouldn't normally come in contact with." We do not have to be afraid. We do not have to wonder what we will say, for He will be with us, and His Holy Spirit will guide our tongues. What will help us through this time the most? Being in communion and constant prayer with our Lord and being in authentic community with other believers. Why do I say *authentic* community? Because it's so easy to be fake in community, but when we do that, we rob ourselves of the chance to grow and be challenged in our walk with the Lord, and being challenged by our brothers and sisters in Christ is the training grounds for the true battle out there in the world. In and of myself, I cannot be ready or even willing to fight these battles. But in Him and His strength, I can overcome. I have to be preparing for these battles, and training comes through linking arms in community and knowing what our Bible says.

He will use those who are willing. I don't have to be anything special. I can fall on my face a million times, but if I say, "Here I am, Lord," He will say, "I will send you." And He will speak through me.

He's on His way. We can see it in the absolutely bonkers times we're living in.

Are we ready for His return? Do we have unbelieving family or friends? I don't know about you, but I've still got some good news to spread.

PRAYER

Lord, please give me the courage to stand for You! Please give me a community of believers to link arms with, to strengthen and prepare for the battles ahead! I pray that You will use my life as You see fit.

....

....

....

....

....

....

....

....

....

....

....

....

....

continue your personal prayer

KEEP MOVING FORWARD

Watch and pray, lest you enter into temptation, the
spirit indeed is willing, but the flesh is weak.
—Mark 14:38

Our only safe place from temptation is being in steadfast prayer, always on the defense, in constant communication with our commander. If we fall asleep or become lazy, we will be destroyed by the enemy. Jesus says to Peter, "I see that you want to be strong. Your spirit is willing, but you're weak in and of yourself. Prayer is the only thing that will keep you strong."

And He says the same to you and me. We must not fall asleep in our spiritual wars. Just because there are no attacks at the moment doesn't mean you are safe. The moment you fall asleep and are no longer on guard is the very moment the enemy will sneak into your camp. There is no idling in our walk with Jesus, no neutral; you're either moving forward in your walk with Jesus or you're falling back. Like being in a rushing river, if you're not fighting the current to move forward, you're sure to be swept away. We must keep fighting the enemy; with Jesus as our strength and prayer as our weapon, the battle is already won.

PRAYER

Jesus, fight for me. Let me not lose heart. Let me never forget where my strength lies. It's You.

BECAUSE OF ENVY

This morning while reading, a tough question came to mind. "Who are you envious of?" I tried to answer, "No one." I guess the problem with having an internal dialogue is you can't fool yourself for too long, and you can't fool the Lord at all. Have you ever met someone who is just so Christlike it kind of makes you envious of them? Like, I want to be that ... kind, generous, genuine. I would argue this type of envy can go one of three ways. It can cause you to slander that person out of envy, cause you to hypocritically emulate that person, or spur real, genuine change.

Sometimes I find myself uncomfortable around those Christians, not because of them but because of my own insecurities and shortcomings. I know myself too well to know I'm not as Christlike as them. It's the flashlight of conviction this person brings to my life. I desire to be more Christlike; I desire to shine in the same way but feel inferior to those who may live more above reproach than I do. I tend to be more of the hypocritical chameleon. I tend to change my personality or actions around those people, somewhat like Peter did when he was with the Jewish Christians in Acts 11:2 and was rebuked by Paul in Galatians 2:11 for being a hypocrite.

In Mark 15:10, it says that the chief priests handed Jesus over because of envy. Sometimes I feel I do this same thing in my heart with people I'm insecure around. I say, "Oh, well she's just too sweet." But in reality, if I was speaking truth, I'd say, "Oh, well she just brings too much conviction into my life." I imagine Jesus brought conviction in much greater ways than any human could. I wonder, if He was alive today, would I avoid Him too? I don't believe I would, so the question is why? is it because I'm more worried about what people think over what Jesus says of me? Is it because Jesus is kinder, more forgiving, and all-knowing? If I wouldn't be ashamed in Jesus's presence, why should I ever be in any human's presence? If I feel like I would be ashamed in the presence of Jesus, maybe it's because I don't fully know or believe what He says of me. He says I am washed white as snow (Isaiah 1:18). I am sanctified (1 Corinthians 6:11). I am called His bride (Hosea 2:19). He loves me in all my messiness. I can stand in confidence because of whose I am. Don't let insecurities keep you from relationships.

It's hard to admit insecurities, but admitting them is the first step to God changing those broken areas in our lives. The first step to Him making us more like Him.

PRAYER

Lord, please take the broken things in me. Show me how my sins have been cleansed through Your blood and how I no longer have to walk in shame. Take my life and fill me with Your Spirit. Make me whole.

....

....

....

....

....

....

....

continue your personal prayer

WE HAVE THE CURE

"Go. And these signs will follow those who believe."
—Mark 16:15

What signs is Jesus talking about here? He's talking about healing and miracles. A common way of thinking nowadays is "Miraculous healings don't really happen anymore." But do you think that could have something to do with our unbelief or maybe indifference to the suffering of the lost around us? Jesus says these signs *will* follow those who believe. Now these healings don't necessarily mean all physical, although they could be physical; we also have the power through Jesus in us to heal hearts and change lives.

If I had a simple pill that was the cure for all cancer, it would be cruel to keep it to myself. I'd be screaming from the rooftops, "Take this pill, and the suffering and death from such a horrible disease will stop!" But I don't have the cure for cancer. I have the cure to eternal death. Let's let that sink in for just a moment. Cancer is one of the worst and most common diseases of our time, but cancer, as painful and terrible as it is, is absolutely nothing compared to *eternal* suffering and *eternal* death, which is how hell is described multiple times by Jesus Himself. Even knowing this fact, I choose to keep this *cure* to myself much of the time.

A quote I once heard (it was actually from a devout atheist talking about the belief of Christians; I don't remember who it was) went something like this: "How much would you have to hate someone to believe that without Jesus they're going to eternally suffer in hell, but still choose to not tell them what you believe the truth is, which would keep them from that?"

I would argue that indifference is the most common sin in the Christian church as a whole. We must pray that Jesus will transform our hearts with love for the lost, that we might better represent the hands and feet of Jesus.

PRAYER

Lord, forgive me of my sin of indifference toward the lost. Stir my heart with true love and let me spread Your Gospel, which is the cure for all brokenness in life.

....

....

....

....

....

....

....

....

....

....

....

continue your personal prayer

RUN TO ME

Shame and regret are some of the enemy's most powerful weapons. The enemy uses both as a tool to drive us from Jesus. He knows if the attack is effective enough, we will run away from our protection and strength. Jesus opens the door to the fortress saying, "Run to Me! I will protect you." But instead, we look at Him, thinking, *Maybe His grace isn't enough this time.* So we run the opposite direction, into the desert, all alone as the enemy helicopter shoots its machine gun of shame down at us. When he has us here, he knows we have no defense.

Jesus knows who we are. He's known since before the foundations of the earth, yet He chose us (Ephesians 1:4). His love for us is like photoshop filters; it blocks out any blemish, leaving only beauty. Before God, we stand blemish-free. He sees His perfect creation through the blood of His Son. Run to Him when the attacks in your mind come. He is our only protection, and in Him we need not live in shame.

> I will Love you, O Lord, my strength. The Lord is my rock and my fortress and my deliverer; My God my strength, in whom I will trust; My strength and the horn of my salvation, my stronghold. I will call upon the Lord who is worthy to be praised. So, I shall be saved from my enemy. (Psalm 18:1–3)

> But God demonstrates His own love toward us, in that while we were still sinners, Christ died for us. (Romans 5:8)

PRAYER

Lord, please remind me how You see me. Forgive me. Let me be quick to repent but also quick to remember I don't have to sulk in my mistakes. You died to forgive every mistake, knowing what I would do long before I was ever born.

continue your personal prayer

THE NEED IS REAL

The times I get off my schedule, I realize how much more I need Jesus. When I don't get my quiet time in the mornings, I notice how much of a sinner I truly am. I don't need His words and guidance just sometimes but all the time. On the days I say, "I don't have time to spend with Him," these are the days I struggle the most; I have no strength, I'm selfish, and I'm tired and empty.

Is it even worth it to not make time for Jesus? I would argue with an emphatic "No." I need to make that time, every day. If I say He's the only thing that matters in life, then I need to make sure He's the purpose driving my actions today. He's the only one who can change me for the better. He's the only one who can change my world. I need to fill myself with His words if I want to make any difference. If I want to battle against the enemy at all, it starts with preparation of my heart. You may be like me and say, "My sphere of influence is not big enough to matter." That's a lie we mustn't believe; if you are able to minister to just one person in a day, heaven rejoices. I can do nothing without Him. Even when I am filled with His Holy Spirit, the battle against my flesh is intense, but without a fresh renewal of His Spirit daily, the battle is far more than I can overcome. I'm reminded every day not to waste one precious moment that could be spent with Him. In the end, when we hear "Well done, good and faithful servant," as we enter the kingdom of God, do you think anything but the time we spent in the presence of God, and the time we spent spreading His Word, will matter even in the slightest?

Blessed is the man
Who walks not in the counsel of the ungodly,
Nor stands in the path of sinners,
Nor sits in the seat of the scornful;
But his delight is in the law of the Lord,
And in His law he meditates day and night.
(Psalm 1:1–2)

PRAYER

Lord, please align my heart with what matters to You. Remind me what is important and what will matter for eternity.

....

....

....

....

....

....

....

....

....

....

continue your personal prayer

WHAT'S IN MY HEART

For out of the abundance of a mans heart his mouth speaks.
—Luke 6:45b

This scripture really convicted me this morning. What kind of water do people want to drink? Clean or stagnant? I learned a new appreciation for clean drinking water while living in Mexico. A few days of violent stomach sickness taught me to be sure of my drinking source.

A well can only pump the water it is filled with. Luke 6:45 made me ask myself, what am I filling myself with—life or death? There is so much putrid *water* being thrown at us daily, and the enemy of our souls calls it entertainment. This *entertainment* is designed to desensitize us to the evil things in this world, and if we're not mindful, we drink it down, not knowing the more we drink, the more danger our souls are in. If we're being filled with poison, poison is all that can flow out.

I've always loved this analogy: Christians are like tea bags; you don't know what flavor they are until they're in hot water. You may be able to hide things that you are filling yourself with until you are facing something "hot" or difficult. Right now, we may be telling ourselves, "I can handle this little bit of filth in this TV show," or "That music isn't a problem." But we may not know the effect of that poison on our souls until we are facing something big, that our souls aren't strong enough in Jesus to overcome. Poison matters; don't let the enemy tell you otherwise.

I must be aware of what I'm filling myself with if I want to be an effective water source that gives life to the thirsty.

PRAYER

Lord, please give my spirit strength to overcome the temptations to fill myself with that which is contrary to You. I need You and nothing else.

....
....
....
....
....
....
....
....
....
....
....
....

continue your personal prayer

THE BIGGER DEBT

"There was a certain creditor who had two debtors. One owed
five hundred denarii, and the other fifty. And when they had
nothing with which to repay, he freely forgave them both.
Tell Me, therefore, which of them will love him more?"
—Luke 7:41–42

Jesus can and will forgive. He loves to forgive people who feel
like they can't be forgiven. Why? Because those who have been
forgiven much love Him that much more. Accept His forgiveness that
is extended to you and to everyone. He loves to use the worst of us
sinners, because after we realize the fullness of His love and forgiveness,
we are more eager to share the good news of what He can do!

It's hard to believe He can and will forgive. I've been in that place
of despair before, believing what the enemy so desperately wants us
to believe, which is "No way. I'm too far gone. I know He's capable,
but I don't believe He's willing to forgive me."

Peter probably believed this lie as well, after denying he ever knew
Jesus in the Gospels. But after Jesus restored Peter, after accepting
Jesus's forgiveness, Peter was used mightily! Peter was a force to be
reckoned with. Peter was all in. Jesus knows that those who know
they are in desperate need of forgiveness—once they take hold of
that forgiveness, once they understand the mountain of debt that has
been removed from their account—will never let it go. They will
love Him all the more.

Our debts are the same across the board. Some people feel that
if they don't have some elaborate testimony, or if they didn't rebel
in some great way, if they weren't "forgiven much," then they can't

love much. That simply isn't true. Sin is sin in God's eyes. Whether you've murdered someone in reality or been angry in your heart and murdered them there, Jesus says this is the same sin (Matthew 5:22). And if you've committed the same sin, you can realize the same forgiveness. That's the key, instead of saying, "Well, I'm pretty good. I'm not that much in debt." You can love the creditor all that much more because you realize what He's forgiven you of!

PRAYER

Jesus, I pray You will reveal to me the extent to which I've been forgiven. Let me love You as the creditor Who's wiped away every debt. You're the reason I'm free.

....

....

....

....

....

....

....

....

....

continue your personal prayer

PETER, JAMES, AND JOHN

These three seemed to be Jesus's favorite disciples. In the Gospels, we see how they are always going with Him to pray, experiencing supernatural things like the transfiguration and walking on water. Why? Why Peter, James, and John? Because they were chosen? Mainly, I would say yes. Jesus uses who He will. But partly I believe He took them along on these special excursions because they chose Him. We see these three choose closeness with Jesus. Peter is maybe the most talkative in the Gospels, showing himself very intimately connected to Jesus. John leans on Jesus at the table (John 13:25) and calls himself, in his own Gospel, multiple times "the disciple whom Jesus loved" (John 13:23, 19:26, 20:2, 21:7, 21:20). This James, not to be confused with the author of the book of James, is not mentioned much in the gospels, but we can assume he was also very much intentionally connected to Jesus. They chose to have an especially intimate relationship; this relationship was open to all the others. But we see that these three chose it. Does that mean Jesus didn't love the others? No. Jesus loved them all. They were His community, His twelve, but He chose to let those three witness things in the journey that the others didn't get to, because they desired to be deeper, closer, and more intimate.

We didn't choose Him; He first chose us. But now that we have Him in our lives, we also have the opportunity to decide. Do we go deeper, or are we content to know Him and walk with Him, but that's it? Jesus will use who He wills, but our willingness and desire to be used is a factor of how much and how elaborate our experience in our walk with Him will be. He wants to show us incredible things, but we first have to choose intimacy with Him. Choose to step out of the boat like Peter. Choose to be close like James and John. Choose to go away with Him and spend the time it takes to know Him deeply. The opportunity is open to all. We have to choose it.

PRAYER

Lord, let me choose You as You have first chosen me. Reveal Yourself deeper to me. Let me be intimately connected to You so that my life can be used for Your glory.

....

....

....

....

....

....

....

....

....

....

continue your personal prayer

SURRENDERED
HEARTS BEFORE
SERVING HANDS

But Martha was distracted with much serving, and she
approached Him and said, "Lord, do You not care that my sister
has left me to serve alone? Therefore tell her to help me."
And Jesus answered and said to her, "Martha, Martha,
you are worried and troubled about many things. But
one thing is needed, and Mary has chosen that good
part, which will not be taken away from her."
—Luke 10:40–42

Serving is good, but worship is better. Jesus doesn't want our busy hands until He first has our surrendered hearts. Works without a love and relationship with Him is empty and worthless. As clanging cymbals are alone just noise (1 Corinthians 13:1–3), so are works without love and a relationship with Jesus. He would much rather have a deep love than a whole bunch of service without purpose.

We see Martha is angry, which shows us a heart problem. If she was serving the Lord with no malice in her heart, we would never have heard about it (surely there were plenty of people serving around Jesus who we never read about). We see that because she's serving, she is judging her sister for not serving. When we serve out of the wrong heart motivation, we can begin to get prideful, and pride leads us to judge others around us for "not doing as much." It's important for me to ask myself, "Why am I serving? Is it for man or for Jesus? Am I doing this to get the recognition for being a good Christian, or am

I doing it out of a true love and relationship with Him?" If it's not the latter, then surely I will receive my empty reward here on earth.

PRAYER

Lord, let my heart be devoted to love You first and foremost. Let me seek Your glory and not my own. Let me love You with all my heart, soul, mind, and strength, and out of that love, let me serve my fellow brothers and sisters.

....

....

....

....

....

....

....

....

....

....

....

continue your personal prayer

NO NEUTRAL GROUND

"He who is not with Me is against Me, and he
who does not gather with me scatters."
—Luke 11:23

Being against Jesus isn't something most of us would cognitively align ourselves or our actions with. Given the blatant choice to "do this thing, which is for God," or "do this thing, which is against Him," most if not all of us would choose the former option. Unfortunately, sometimes life isn't that straightforward.

There's no neutral ground. Jesus says, "If it's not for Me, it's against Me." There are so many things out there in this world today that we think of as neutral, a gray area, and in and of themselves, they might be, but the way those things affect us is either for Jesus and pushing us closer, or against Him and pulling us away. The simplest distractions might not be by themselves evil. (Some are evil. Ever watch *that* movie that by the end of it, you just want to take a shower? Be especially aware of those things, for those things sear the conscience, and they blur the lines between good and evil within our souls.)

Anytime we let something take priority from our time spent in the Word or in the presence of Jesus, those things that were just simple distractions have become things that are against Jesus. Plain and simple, just to drive the point home, we're either for Him or against Him, either furthering His kingdom or our own. No middle ground, no neutral safe haven. We're either swimming upstream or drifting with the current, and you know who drifts with the current? Dead fish. It's time we choose. Choose to give Him *all* of our life as a living sacrifice, not just bits and pieces. Not having a compartmentalized life. Choose to gather with Him, to live in abundance of life, knowing our life is His. He dwells in us, which means we take Him with us wherever we go. So where are we going to go?

PRAYER

Lord, take all of my life. Direct my thoughts, desires, decisions, and entertainment. Let everything I fill myself with be glorifying to You and edifying to me. With Your strength, I'll be able to swim upstream.

....

....

....

....

....

....

....

....

....

continue your personal prayer

WHY DO WE FEAR PEOPLE MORE THAN GOD?

"And I say to you, My friends, do not be afraid of those who kill the body, and after that have no more that they can do. But I will show you whom you should fear: Fear Him who, after He has killed, has power to cast into hell; yes, I say to you, fear Him!"
—Luke 12:4–5

If we grasp hold of the true power offered to us through the Holy Spirit, we can be so bold knowing that man has no power over us. Truly, what can man do to us anyway? If we are in Christ, just as Paul says, and I paraphrase, in Philippians 1:21, "To live is Christ's Word being spread; to die is to be in eternity with Him." First of all, there may come a day when we might face deadly persecution, but nowadays, death is a very extreme example. Being laughed at or screamed at is probably close to the worst a normal Christian will face in our society. But it's very good to realize that death really is the worst thing a person could do, and if we're in Christ, we don't have to fear death! It's a win-win; we live to spread the Gospel and therefore store up our treasures in heaven. If we die, it's truly a gain. This begs two questions. First, am I living to spread the Gospel? Second, do I believe that death is a gain?

If I grasp hold of the truest life calling, both the answers to these questions would be yes. But how easy is it to go about my day checking off the to-do list, only to get to the end of the day and realize I did nothing to further God's kingdom today. If I'm not living to spread the Gospel, I won't be living in the abundant life Jesus promises us, and more than likely, I'll be scared. Scared of people and scared of death.

Knowing this truth, I then have to ask myself, why do I tend to fear people's opinion of me? I mean, there should be a reverence of how well I'm representing Jesus in me, but how much more I should concern myself with God's opinion of me. I should worry more about how God sees me and being right in His eyes than anyone else's. How quickly I can get distracted by the things I've got going here on earth when I should be worried about growing His kingdom in heaven. I'm not important. I cannot do anything good unless He uses me; only then am I of any good to anybody.

If my sins are covered in Jesus's blood, I'm perfect in the sight of God, and no one else's opinion matters. I can stand boldly, unafraid. Today's reading comes with a challenge: tell someone who doesn't know about your faith today. The more you tell, the more your courage will grow and the less you'll fear people. You're on your way to fearing only God!

PRAYER

Lord, fill me today with Your courage through Your Holy Spirit. Let me be bold in reverencing only You! Let my love grow for You and those around me who are lost.

....

....

....

....

continue your personal prayer

WE ALL SERVE SOMEBODY

Do you not know that to whom you present yourselves slaves to
obey, you are that one's slaves whom you obey, whether of sin
leading to death, or of obedience leading to righteousness? But
God be thanked that though you were slaves of sin, yet you obeyed
from the heart that form of doctrine to which you were delivered.
—Romans 6:16–17

We like to think of ourselves as independent; we're not a slave
to anyone or anything. No one likes to be told what to do.
In fact, I'd say that's one of the main reasons people steer clear of
religion in general, especially Christianity. "I don't want a bunch of
rules to follow. I don't want to be slave to anyone."

When someone does drugs, are they a slave to that drug? When
someone has an addiction of any kind, do they own that addiction
or does the addiction own them?

Of course the addiction owns them. The only difference between
Jesus or an addiction ruling your life is one loves you (Jesus, who
laid down His life for you), and the other wants to destroy you and
see you burn in hell for eternity (Satan, a.k.a. the father of addiction
and lies). Which master would you rather serve?

If your life is not surrendered to Jesus, I guarantee you struggle
with some form of addiction. We were created to worship, to be
subject to Christ. We were created for a fulfilled and euphoric life,
which is only found in serving and living for Jesus. When we reject
Him, something has to fill that void. In place of Jesus, we worship

sex, drugs, adrenaline, or food, something to make us feel alive, but at the end of all of those things, we're left feeling empty and only longing more. Why is that? Because the answer to all emptiness is Jesus. Perfect creation had us in constant communion, walking in the garden with God. Sin entered and broke every bit of the design He had for us. Sin keeps us from that community with Him. But praise Him for Jesus, who covered us in His blood. Now, because of that veil, God only sees His Son, and we can be in right relationship with God our Father.

If you haven't given Him full access to your life, if you're reading this and longing for stronger purpose, give Him your whole heart today. Watch as He changes every aspect throughout your walk. Then go share your faith. There is nothing more euphoric or adrenaline inducing than that.

PRAYER

Lord, I thank You for the blood of Jesus. He is the only reason I can stand before You at all. I believe He died on the cross for my sins and that He rose again on the third day. He is now seated on the throne with You in heaven. I want You to have all of my heart, every bit. Please transform my life like only You can do. Renew and take the things away that don't glorify You.

....

....

....

....

....

continue your personal prayer

SPRING OF LIFE

If anyone comes to Me and does not hate his father and
mother, wife and children, brothers and sisters, yes,
and his own life also, he cannot be My disciple.
—Luke 14:26

Wait—what? I thought we were supposed to love, not hate.
Well, Jesus is actually talking about loving Him above all
else, so much so that in comparison to these other beloved people
in our lives, it would look like hate. It's about being so obedient to
Him that if anyone or anything tried to pull us away from Him to
do something contrary, we would only listen to the Holy Spirit in us.

Jesus is using this word *hate* to really drive home a point. He
wants us to understand the level of commitment He desires from us.
No matter what comes, no matter what family issues arise, and no
matter who we lose in this life, His desire is for us to be so close and
intimately connected that we are able to say, maybe even with tears
in our eyes, "I'm still choosing You, Lord."

Once we fully understand His heart toward us, this level of
love and commitment is really the easiest heart decision of all.
He's our comfort through every storm. Unlike any level of human
commitment we will ever experience, He will never walk away. He
will never mess up, and He is always faithful, even when we're not.
We can always count on Him. Why wouldn't we commit our lives
fully to Him and no one else? If our cup is being filled, we can pour
out to our family, our spouse, our kids, and our friends. But we're not
expecting them to fill us back up; we've already got a never-ending
spring of life, and His name is Jesus. Commit fully to Him today.

PRAYER

Lord, help me to fully choose You! Every hour, my heart needs to be reminded who I'm living for. I'm so fickle, and my heart is so deceitfully wicked, yet You are steadfast. You love me fully. You never let go. Train my heart to be devoted fully to You. Let my eyes be fixed on You!

....

....

....

....

....

....

....

....

....

....

....

....

....

continue your personal prayer

HEAVEN REJOICES

Luke, chapter 15, is all about reconciliation—the lost being found and how God and all of heaven rejoice. We tend to think as the prodigal son did, that we're going to have to make excuses and have a speech ready for when we get home.

> "Father I have sinned against heaven and before you, and I am no longer worthy to be called your son. Make me like one of your hired servants." (Luke 15:18b–19)

The reality is as soon as we turn around and start heading home, our Father runs out to meet us. Repentance is simply the act of turning and heading home, and as soon as repentance takes place, restoration happens. The son was immediately restored to his position. There was no testing process. The father didn't say, "We'll see if you stick around this time." He didn't say, "Okay, let's hear your speech. What do you have to say for yourself?" No, he said, "This is my son. He's back. Put my robe and ring on him, and let's have a party."

How gracious, forgiving, and loving our Father is. I'm so thankful that He has forgiven me! As much as the enemy would like us to believe it, we're never too far gone to turn back to Him. He's right behind you with open arms. Just look at how tender our heavenly Father is. There's no cross attitude, no snarky comment, just genuine happiness for the return of His lost child.

Whether it's forgiveness we need to accept or extend, I think there's a lesson here for every one of us. Be gracious as our heavenly Father is gracious.

PRAYER

Lord, please let my heart know You. Let me accept Your forgiveness and extend that same forgiveness to others. Let Your Word penetrate deep in my heart and change me from the inside out.

....

....

....

....

....

....

....

....

....

....

....

....

....

continue your personal prayer

FOREVER IS A
LONG TIME

> There was a certain rich man who was clothed in purple and
> fine linen and fared sumptuously every day. But there was a
> certain beggar named Lazarus, full of sores, who was laid at his
> gate, desiring to be fed with the crumbs which fell from the
> rich man's table. Moreover the dogs came and licked his sores.
> So it was that the beggar died and was carried by the angels
> to Abraham's bosom. The rich man also died and was
> buried. And being in torments in Hades, he lifted up his
> eyes and saw Abraham afar off, and Lazarus in his bosom.
> Then he cried and said, "Father Abraham, have mercy on
> me, and send Lazarus that he may dip the tip of his finger in
> water and cool my tongue; for I am tormented in this flame."
> But Abraham said, "Son, remember that in your lifetime
> you received your good things, and likewise Lazarus evil
> things; but now he is comforted, and you are tormented."
> —Luke 16:19–25

First, I just want to point out that in the printed Word of God,
these words are in red, which means Jesus is telling this account.
Hell is a very real place, and Jesus is telling these graphic details to
keep us from experiencing hell for ourselves.

I've heard many people ignorantly joke that they're going to
go "party in hell when they die." That statement couldn't be more
false. What we read here is a gruesome picture of just how bad hell
is. It is a very real, very dark, very torturous place where people will

long for a drop of water on their tongue for relief and *never* get that relief. My finite mind has a hard time grasping forever, but forever is a very long time.

The second thing I'd like to touch on here is how the earthly state of a man's life is far less important than the eternal state. Just because a person has little in the way of earthy possessions doesn't mean they're poor, and likewise, having a lot here on earth doesn't necessarily mean you're rich. Sure, there is a net worth that can be measured, but a great net worth without Jesus is bankruptcy in the life to come.

Lazarus had far more riches than the rich man, spiritually speaking. If we are in a position to help and we see a person who is poor and in need of basic necessities to live, we are called to be the hands and feet of Jesus and to give to those who ask (Luke 6:30). But more important than earthly possessions, we need to look at the state of our spiritual account, and we need to make sure we are even more concerned with where people spend eternity. We may be able to give earthly riches, but no matter our net worth on this earth, if we're in Christ, we have the same spiritual riches to share with all in need. Personally, I'd rather live in poverty on earth, storing up riches for eternity, than the other way around.

PRAYER

Lord, let me be spiritually rich in Your grace and love. Thank You that my name is written in Your Book of Life. I get to go to heaven because of Your sacrifice and the grace poured out for me. I get to go to heaven because of Your free gift. Let me share with others the riches of a life spent with You.

....

....

continue your personal prayer

TRULY, WHICH WAS WHICH?

Continuing through this account of where the rich man and poor man eventually end up for eternity, we soon have to ask which is which? Which man is rich and which is poor?

Just because people are blessed and have possessions doesn't mean they are doomed to hell. But as we see earlier in this chapter and other places in the Bible, you cannot serve two masters (Luke 16:13), and the love of money is the root of all evil (1 Timothy 6:10). We can be blessed with money, but money is a really terrible god. Where man's treasure lies, there his heart will be also (Matthew 6:21). We must be careful to not let our possessions possess our hearts. For they won't help us when we leave this earth.

> And besides all this, between us and you there is a great gulf fixed, so that those who want to pass from here to you cannot, nor can those from there pass to us. (Luke 16:26)

I believe this is saying people in hell will be able to see the people in heaven. They will long to be there but won't be able to.

I've heard people say, "How can a loving God send people to hell?" Are you kidding? God sent His Son so that no one would go to hell! No, if people go to hell, it's because people choose to go to hell by rejecting Jesus and His free gift of life.

Then he said, "I beg you therefore, father, that you would send him to my father's house, for I have five brothers, that he may testify to them, lest they also come to this place of torment." (Luke 16:27–28)

"Please go tell my family not to come here. This is no party; there is nothing good about this place."

Abraham said to him, "They have Moses and the prophets; let them hear them." And he said, "No, father Abraham; but if one goes to them from the dead, they will repent." But he said to him, "If they do not hear Moses and the prophets, neither will they be persuaded though one rise from the dead." (Luke 16:29–31)

They have everything they need to be able to make a choice. They have all the prophecy and evidence. Not making a choice to walk this life with Jesus *is* making the choice to spend eternity in hell. Don't wait to make that decision for yourself, and don't wait to tell the ones you love. None of us know our life span, but even eighty, ninety, or 110 years is but the blink of an eye in comparison with eternity.

For since the creation of the world His invisible attributes are clearly seen, being understood by the things that are made, even His eternal power and Godhead, so that they are without excuse, because, although they knew God, they did not glorify Him as God, nor were thankful, but became futile in their thoughts, and their foolish hearts were darkened. Professing to be wise, they became fools, and changed the glory of the incorruptible God into an image made like corruptible man—and birds and four-footed animals and creeping things. (Romans 1:20–23)

We are given all the evidence we need to make a choice. We can look around at beautiful creation itself. The sun is the perfect distance from the earth to make everything work. The earth is tilted just right. The birds chirping help the plants to grow. Plants take in carbon dioxide and give off oxygen. Mammals breathe in oxygen and breathe out carbon dioxide. Everything works together perfectly; this design tells of its designer, God. We don't need any more evidence. If we reject God, it's not because we didn't have a choice, it's simply because our rebellious nature didn't accept God as our designer, for if we accept Him as the designer, we have to submit to His design. Plain and simple, my friend reading this, if you still choose not to submit your life to Jesus, it's because you did *choose* to reject Him, and now, because you read this, you are completely without excuse. So now choose wisely.

If you've been walking with Jesus for two seconds or for ninety years, I'm happy to be your sister in Christ. Let this be a reminder to spread the Gospel with the lost today.

PRAYER

Lord, give me words to speak Your truth. Fill me with the Holy Spirit and reveal Yourself to me anew in this moment. Keep me from evil. Let me spread Your truth in love.

....

....

....

....

....

continue your personal prayer

WE MUST BE CAREFUL

> Then He said to the disciples, "It is impossible that no
> offenses should come, but woe to him through whom they
> do come! It would be better for him if a millstone were
> hung around his neck, and he were thrown into the sea,
> than that he should offend one of these little ones."
> —Luke 17:1–2

In the NIV, it says woe to him who causes anyone to stumble. We must stand for truth, so we will be offensive to people from time to time. But we must be careful not to cause someone to stumble. Paul says if eating meat would cause my brother to stumble, I would never eat meat again (1 Corinthians 8:13). Just because something isn't sin for you doesn't mean it may not cause your brothers or your sisters in the faith any harm. If there is a conviction, that is God saying, "I don't want you to do that." What you're doing may not, in and of itself, be sinful. But if God says not to, and you do it anyway, that is when it becomes sin in your life. It can be different for every person, based on personal struggle and conviction. What is not sin for you may be a big struggle or conviction for me based on past experiences, or maybe even the point I'm at in my walk with Jesus. That's why Philippians 2:12 tells us to work out our own salvation with fear and trembling. We're not to pass judgment on anyone for their own convictions. God judges their heart; we can only judge their fruit, the same way we can tell an apple tree by its fruit. We can get some idea of who our brothers are in Christ, but a baby apple tree is still an apple tree even if it hasn't budded yet, the same way we need to be very careful judging the fruit of our brother, not knowing where they are in their growth. We are to live a quiet life, mind our own business, and work with our hands (1 Thessalonians 4:11–13), because if we're honest, we have enough of our own problems.

PRAYER

Lord, let me live life in honor of You. Let me live in quiet conviction. Let me work out my own faith and live only to please You. You alone deserve the honor and praise.

....

....

....

....

....

....

....

....

....

....

continue your personal prayer

HUMBLED OR EXALTED

Everyone who exalts himself will be humbled, and
he who humbles himself will be exalted.
—Luke 18:14b

I'd much rather be exalted than humbled, for being humbled means
being humiliated. I exalt myself when I forget that I was saved
impossibly by a God who can do the impossible. I forget the gift He gave
me and start to think I got this on my own. I must always remember He
did it and is still doing it now. There's never a point at which He hands
life over to me and says, "Okay, you're trained. You're an expert! You
can do it now." Nope. I am a mess when I try to do it on my own. I
need his guidance daily, minutely, by the very millisecond, and anytime
I think that statement is dramatic or overkill, I get humbled quickly. I
must pray that He always remains in His place of authority in my life.
He's in the pilot seat. I'm lucky to be the one handing out snacks. I must
never forget the gift of salvation He freely gave to me.

Pride or exaltation of myself has no place in my life when I
remember where I'd be, where I was, without Him.

PRAYER

Lord, be in Your place of exaltation today and let me take the
humblest seat. Thank You for Your grace extended to me, which
saved me and is still reconciling me to You. I will not have spiritually
arrived anywhere close to perfection until I see You face-to-face in
heaven. Let me never exalt myself.

WHAT I'M FILLED WITH

Finally, brethren, whatever things are true, whatever
things *are* noble, whatever things *are* just, whatever things
are pure, whatever things *are* lovely, whatever things
are of good report, if *there is* any virtue and if *there is*
anything praiseworthy—meditate on these things.
—Philippians 4:8

There isn't much in the way of entertainment these days that fit these criteria. I even argue that there isn't anything truly entertaining that matches these criteria perfectly. We must be careful, for what we fill ourselves with is surely what will come out. A vessel can only pour out what it's filled with. If we're filling ourselves with things contrary to Jesus and His Word, the probability that we will pour out those things is not just probable; it's sure.

Now let's look at the contents in our heart as a jar of homemade salad dressing. We mix some vinegar (we'll have this represent things of this world), olive oil, and spices (this can represent the things of the Holy Spirit). (This might not be the best analogy considering you would want to shake up salad dressing, but let's just roll with it.) If I don't shake up my homemade salad dressing, I can pretty easily pour off the oil and spices that are floating on top. I can pour out spiritual things pretty easily, for they are right on the surface. But when life gets all mixed up, when I go through tough challenges or when I'm tested, the evil in my heart can start to get mixed in and unintentionally spill out.

It would be best to just heed this scripture and many others like it, choosing to fill ourselves with things that align with the character of Jesus. Then the sour, bitter things that don't mix well with Him who lives in us don't even exist in the bottom of our hearts. They have no way of rearing their ugly heads when we least expect it.

PRAYER

Lord, free me from the things of this world. I so desire to be filled with only You. Give me more of Your Holy Spirit as I walk with you daily.

....

....

....

....

....

....

....

....

....

....

continue your personal prayer

HE'S COMING

But when you hear of wars and commotions, do
not be terrified; for these things must come to pass
first, but the end *will* not *come* immediately.
—Luke 21:9

Right now, I think we can all agree there's a lot of commotion. I don't like watching the news, as I tend to get very fired up and frustrated. I say, "Obviously legalizing drugs, defunding police departments, and trying to pay off the weather so it won't change are all very bad ideas. Can't these people use their brains?" Well, in all reality, they can't; they're blinded for the sake of the Gospel. In order for these things to come into being, and in order for Jesus's plan to unfold, these things must happen. It is all in God's plan, and it should excite those of us who'll meet Him in the clouds (1 Thess. 4:17)! And it should concern those who aren't positive they are going. If you're not sure you're going with Him, you can be sure right this second. But please make that choice before it's too late, as we keep reading this chapter. We can be certain we don't want to be here for the great tribulation.

> And there will be signs in the sun, in the moon, and in the stars; and on the earth distress of nations, with perplexity, the sea and the waves roaring; men's hearts failing them from fear and the expectation of those things which are coming on the earth, for the powers of the heavens will be shaken. Then they will see the Son of Man coming in a cloud with power and great

glory. Now when these things begin to happen, look up and lift up your heads, because your redemption draws near. (Luke 21:25–28)

"Men's hearts failing from fear." That sure doesn't sound like a place I want to be. With that said, I'm a pretribulation rapture believer. In other words, I believe that the church, which is made up of the born-again believers of Jesus Christ, will not be here. We will be taken to heaven before this takes place. This particular section of scripture is speaking of Jesus's second coming. Some people believe differently, and I know it's a very divisive topic. I'm not going to be dogmatic about it, but that's what I believe, and I have many reasons to back that up, but I can go into that at a later date. Whether Jesus comes back before, in the middle, or at the end of the tribulation, the important thing is He's coming back, and our hearts need to be right before Him. And the only way we can be right before Him is if we repent from our sins and accept His salvation.

Then He spoke to them a parable: "Look at the fig tree, and all the trees. When they are already budding, you see and know for yourselves that summer is now near. So you also, when you see these things happening, know that the kingdom of God is near. Assuredly, I say to you, this generation will by no means pass away till all things take place. Heaven and earth will pass away, but My words will by no means pass away. "But take heed to yourselves, lest your hearts be weighed down with carousing, drunkenness, and cares of this life, and that Day come on you unexpectedly. For it will come as a snare on all those who dwell on the face of the whole earth. Watch therefore, and pray always that you may be counted worthy to escape all these things that will come to pass, and to stand before the Son of Man." (Luke 21:29–36)

Let us live looking for our sweet Jesus's return. Let's not be distracted by the things of this world, but let's be about our Father's business, living for what truly matters, winning hearts with His love and growing His kingdom. The souls of our fellow believers are the only things coming with us to heaven.

PRAYER

Lord, I pray that You will rid my mind of all other unnecessary distractions and help me focus solely on Your mission for my life. Let me be looking for Your return and not be bogged down by things that don't matter. Let me live entirely to know You and make You known.

....

....

....

....

....

....

....

....

....

....

continue your personal prayer

REPENTANCE IN THE FAILURE

And the Lord said, "Simon, Simon! Indeed, Satan has
asked for you, that he may sift *you* as wheat. But I have
prayed for you, that your faith should not fail; and when
you have returned to *Me,* strengthen your brethren."
But he said to Him, "Lord, I am ready to go
with You, both to prison and to death."
—Luke 22:31–33

Just before Jesus goes to the cross, He tells Peter, "There will be
a test, and you are going to fail, but that failure will be used for
My purposes."

Peter might have been a little arrogant when he said, "I'll go
to prison or even death," but I believe he said it with sincerity. He
loved Jesus so much he couldn't imagine denying Him. He believed
in his own human strength that he would be able to stand with Him
till the bitter end. I've been in this place before, on the mountaintop
with Jesus, truly believing with all my heart that I was committed
to Him even to death.

> Then He said, "I tell you, Peter, the rooster shall not
> crow this day before you will deny three times that
> you know Me." (Luke 22:34)

Skipping ahead twenty verses …

Having arrested Him, they led Him and brought Him into the high priest's house. But Peter followed at a distance. Now when they had kindled a fire in the midst of the courtyard and sat down together, Peter sat among them. (Luke 22:54–55)

Notice it says, "Peter followed at a distance ..." As a believer, I think the worst place we can be is at a distance. When our lines aren't clear, when people don't know emphatically that we belong to Jesus, we can begin to compromise, and Satan can use compromise to push us further down a path of failure. "You did that, so they will never believe you love Jesus. Might as well keep hiding it ..."

Peter then sits among *them,* warming himself at the fire. Who does he sit among? He's sitting with the scoffers, the unbelievers. When he was sitting with his fellow disciples and Jesus, he had all the strength in the world, "Jesus, You're out of Your mind! I will not deny You. How could I? You're Jesus! You're sitting here in front of me! Even if I have to die, I will stay with You." But when he was separated, scared and among unbelievers, he found his strength was gone, and he did the very thing he wholeheartedly believed he would never do. First Corinthians 15:33 tells us,

Do not be deceived: "Evil company corrupts good habits."

We must be careful who we surround ourselves with, but more importantly, we must remain close to Jesus. There is good news. When we find ourselves in this place, like to Peter, Jesus says, "Return to me, I will use this failure in your life, to strengthen your brothers" (Luke 22:32b).

I believe I'm the brother (or sister) Jesus is telling Peter about here. I am very encouraged by this account. Even if we've messed up, we can be forgiven and used powerfully! Peter goes on to be a mighty leader of the early church and instrumental in its growth. We can return to Jesus; we've never messed up too badly.

He is always waiting with open arms for us to return to Him in repentance.

PRAYER

Lord, let me be quick to repent and turn to You. In times of failure on my part, let me remember just how forgiving You are. The price has already been paid. I can repent and return.

....

....

....

....

....

....

....

....

....

....

....

continue your personal prayer

JUST THAT SIMPLE

"That if you confess with your mouth the Lord
Jesus and believe in your heart that God has raised
Him from the dead, you will be saved."
—Romans 10:9

In Luke chapter 23, Jesus is hung on the cross in between two thieves. We see one mocks Him, and the other simply says, "Remember me when You get to your kingdom." And we see that Jesus answers him saying, "Today you will be with Me in paradise."

He didn't say, "Let's get you off this cross, get you baptized, take some communion, do some good deeds, test you out a little, and then we'll see. Maybe you'll be good enough to make it to heaven." No, it was as simple as saying, "I deserve death (showing a repentant heart), but I know You are the Son of God (confessing with the mouth). Remember me when You get to heaven (believing with his heart)." And that's all it took. Jesus tells him, "Today you will be with me in heaven."

You know, I think we make this whole Christianity thing much harder than it needs to be. We place burdens on ourselves and others that Jesus never intended us to have. We must look a certain way, act a certain way, be a certain way. And yes, as we grow in maturity, we will change and look more like Him. The difference is we will change naturally, not out of the old boot straps mentality but because spending time with Jesus changes us. Jesus tells us we will judge our brothers and sisters by their fruit, so by being a born-again Christian, you will produce fruit. If you're not, there's a problem, but being born again, you will produce fruit *naturally*. You don't see an apple tree out in the garden straining and striving to pop out an apple, or a grape vine shaking and grunting to produce grapes. Plants produce fruit naturally when they are connected to the vine.

> Jesus tells us "I am the vine, you *are* the branches. He who abides in Me, and I in him, bears much fruit; for without Me you can do nothing." (John 15:5)

Like a branch on a tree, we just hang on to Him. He does everything else. The branch of a tree dies if it is cut off from the trunk; it can't survive, produce fruit, or do anything without its source of life. The same is true for us; we must remain in Him (and that is all we must do), or we too will die.

PRAYER

Lord, simplify my relationship with You in my mind. Let me remain in You and abide in You.

....

....

....

....

....

....

....

continue your personal prayer

THE ANT FARM

Ever feel like a failure? Like you don't measure up? Like you've blown it? Yeah ... it's because you have. The world likes to tell us, "You do you." "You're perfect just the way you are." That's not the truth, and lies only allow you to live in darkness longer. The truth is you are a sinner. You are not good enough to make it to heaven on your deeds. You are dirty. If you died, there's no hope you'd get into heaven in and of yourself. That's the bad news.

The good news is Jesus Christ came. He died and took the punishment we deserve on Himself. Think about that.

Let's put it this way. My dad uses this analogy a lot. Imagine you get an ant farm with your son, and you get a whole bunch of ants. Your son and you raise them, and then you set them free in your front yard. You feed them, and you and your son nurture them and care for them. Then one day, you get the call that the exterminator is coming, so you try to communicate with your ants that they need to come to you, come back to the ant farm, so you can protect them, but they can't hear or understand you because you're too big. So you ask your son to become an ant to warn them. He says, "Because of my love for you and for them, I will become an ant." You watch as he talks to them. you see that some of the ants listen to him and come to the ant farm to be protected, but most reject him, saying, "You're just an ant. How could you possibly know anything more than us?" And eventually, they kill him, so you raise your son and turn him back into a man, but now you can't verbally communicate with your ants anymore. Now as the father, what do you do? Even though you love your ants, you've done all that you can to save them from the exterminator. Now you just have to sit back and hope that your ants come to the ant farm to be protected.

This is a silly analogy compared to what God has done for us, but it gives us a pretty good idea of what Jesus did for us. He told us the truth. Now it's our decision to accept His words and come to the ant farm or not. The gift is free to all.

PRAYER

Thank You, Lord, for Your great grace and love! Thank You for paying for my sins on the cross and providing a way for me to be saved from my depravity.

....

....

....

....

....

....

....

....

....

continue your personal prayer

LOVE

Love is one of the most overused words in the English language. There's only one word, and it can mean many different things. When said to a person, usually the definition behind it is "I have a need, and you're fulfilling that need." This could be emotional, sexual, or physical (money in the pockets, food on the table, etc.).

"I love you" could mean I like the way you make me feel, a feeling. Or "I love" could be a hamburger, a milkshake, a phone, or any inanimate object that you like a lot. But almost always in our society, "I love you" are words we use to get, or because we're getting something from someone else (emotional, physical, or sexual).

The main problem with this form of love is it's innately selfish and based on how you or I feel. So when love is focused on receiving and not focused on serving someone else, if I'm no longer receiving, logic says, "It's time to go," which means if someone hurts my feelings or hard times come and I no longer feel good, then I must be falling out of love with that person.

This is how we treat God most times as well. If He is pouring into me and I hear His voice, I'm good. I'm in love with Him. But if it's all selfish and about what I can get from Him, the second a trial comes, "I'm not sure about this God thing. I don't really know if He is good. I'm not really feeling it."

There's almost no such thing as unconditional love in our society today. Sure, there are wedding vows. People say, "For better or worse, in sickness and in health …" but hardly anyone really means it. Most people should rewrite their vows and say, "Let's test this thing out. I'm not positive that this will work, but you make me feel good, so I'll try." This form of wedding vows is a lot less romantic, huh? But it's true in many cases. Unconditional love does not fail, but unconditional love does not exist without the author of love, Jesus Christ, at the center of both people in the relationship. Love is a choice. Sure, there are going to be those little butterflies, those moments when you *feel* love. But true love is choosing someone no matter how they treat you or act toward you. God doesn't love you only on the occasions when you're treating Him well. In fact, He died for the very people nailing Him to the cross. Remembering this and what true unconditional love looks like will help me to humble myself and love people in my own life so much better.

> But God demonstrates His own love toward us, in that while we were still sinners, Christ died for us. (Romans 5:8)

PRAYER

Lord, if I haven't already, let me have an encounter with Your unconditional love. Give me unconditional, selfless love toward the people in my life. Be my source of life so I can pour that life and love into others.

....

....

....

....

....

....

continue your personal prayer

I CAN ONLY
IMAGINE

There are times when I feel a sense of dullness when getting into the Word. This usually happens when there's not a lot challenging me in life.

I love exercise, so I'm going to use a workout analogy. Let's say I go to the gym and do the same workout routine for months—same movement, same weight, same number of reps every single time, day after day. Pretty soon, that that workout will become easy, as my muscles will have adapted to this movement. Now, it's not a bad thing to be in a season of maintaining where I'm at in my physical strength, but I can't expect my muscles to grow unless I put more strain on them. In a health journey, there are going to be seasons of growth and gains, and there will be seasons of simply maintaining. This is the season when I might take more rest days. But if I say during the maintenance season, "Well, I'm not seeing any growth, so I'm just going to perpetually rest," I can be sure to find that slowly, over time, all my strength will disappear.

The same thing is true of our spiritual journey. There will be seasons. Sometimes we will see exponential growth, and sometimes we will only be maintaining. It's easy to let our guard down during these times. Everything is basically good; no real worries. We'll just rest. But too much rest, just like with physical muscles, can result in atrophy of our spiritual muscles. If we're not diligent in our pursuit of Jesus during the easy times, when tragedies or tests arise, we may look up and realize we've been lulled to sleep and our strength is gone. If we only draw close to God during the times of need and heartache, we have a chance of being caught off guard by the attacks of the enemy. Don't get me wrong. Nothing we do earns our salvation, but our strength comes from pulling closer to Him. We need to praise Him during the good and the bad. Stay close to Him even when things are easy. He is our only strength. We don't want to get caught off guard.

> Watch therefore, for you know neither the day nor the hour in which the Son of Man is coming. (Matthew 25:13)

PRAYER

Lord, please draw me close to You! Increase my strength in all the seasons of life. Let me pull closer to You. Your love alone is my strength.

....

....

....

....

....

....

....

....

continue your personal prayer

DO YOU WANT
TO BE HEALED?

Now there is in Jerusalem by the Sheep *Gate* a pool, which
is called in Hebrew, Bethesda, having five porches. In these
lay a great multitude of sick people, blind, lame, paralyzed,
waiting for the moving of the water. For an angel went down
at a certain time into the pool and stirred up the water; then
whoever stepped in first, after the stirring of the water, was made
well of whatever disease he had. Now a certain man was there
who had an infirmity thirty-eight years. When Jesus saw him
lying there, and knew that he already had been *in that condition*
a long time, He said to him, "Do you want to be made well?"
—John 5:2–6

"Do you want to be healed?"

This seems like a rather obvious answer, Jesus. He's a man
who has been sick for thirty-eight years. He's lying by the pool of
healing to be healed. I think he wants to be healed. Personally,
I think He asks this question to you and me as well. He asks the
question because sometimes we say, "I want to be healed," but in
reality, our actions say differently, because we don't come to the
healer. We continue to stay where we're hurt time and time again.
We stay sick because we don't actually want to be healed; If we did,
we'd go to the Great Physician. We want life, we know we do, but
in a way, we hide behind our infirmity. We say, "I'm too sick to be
healed." We use it as an excuse, much like the man in the next verse.

The sick man answered Him, "Sir, I have no man
to put me into the pool when the water is stirred up;
but while I am coming, another steps down before
me." (John 5:7)

Like this sick man, I also have all these excuses for why I can't
be healed. I live in my infirmity because I refuse to fully give it over
to the Lord and allow Him to heal me. Instead, I try with no avail
to fix myself. There's nothing we can do to heal ourselves; we can
only give it to Him.

Jesus said to him, "Rise, take up your bed and walk."
And immediately the man was made well, took up his
bed, and walked. (John 5:8–9)

It truly is that simple with Jesus. In other miracles, we see that
it takes at least a tiny bit of that person's faith. I think this account
is amazing because this man doesn't say, "Yes, please. Heal me." Or
"Yes, Lord, I believe." This man doesn't have a clue who is standing
before him. It doesn't rely on his faith at all. Jesus can and will heal
who He wants to heal. It is that simple. All He has to do is speak. If
He can heal a man who is not asking for it, how much more can He
heal our hearts if we just simply ask?

PRAYER

Lord, I pray for Your healing. I know that You are the God of
miracles. Help me seek You to heal me.

....

....

continue your personal prayer

HEALING ON
THE SABBATH

> And that day was the Sabbath. The Jews therefore
> said to him who was cured, "It is the Sabbath; it
> is not lawful for you to carry your bed."
> He answered them, "He who made me well said
> to me, 'Take up your bed and walk.'"
> —John 5:9b–11

"I'm healed, guys. I don't really care what's lawful. After thirty-eight years, I'm walking because of that guy, so I'm gonna obey Him. I'm going home."

> Then they asked him, "Who is the Man who said to you, 'Take up your bed and walk'?" But the one who was healed did not know who it was, for Jesus had withdrawn, a multitude being in that place. (John 5:12–13)

This man was not looking for healing, He didn't even know who Jesus was, but he obeyed Him anyway. All he knew was he was healed.

> Afterward Jesus found him in the temple, and said to him, "See, you have been made well. Sin no more, lest a worse thing come upon you." (John 5:14)

Jesus healed him and then revealed who He is. He healed him physically, then took care of him spiritually. He said, "Don't sin anymore. It's for your own good."

The man departed and told the Jews that it was Jesus who had made him well. He simply witnessed and proclaimed what he knew to be true, that Jesus healed him. That's all we're called to do as well! We try to make it complicated in our heads. We say, "Well, I'm no scholar. I don't know the Bible well enough." Do you know that you've been healed from your sin? That doesn't mean that you're perfect or that you never mess up but that your Savior has taken that sin on Himself. None of us know everything. Proclaim what you do know! I've been healed!

PRAYER

Lord, let all the religious stuff fall off. Let us be set free to walk in Your healing, to proclaim Your truth! You have healed me!

....

....

....

....

....

....

....

....

continue your personal prayer

NOT JUST EATING

I seem to think if I'm just reading the Bible, I will magically, automatically be strong. And yes, if we don't eat the meat of the Bible, our spirit, much like our physical bodies if we don't eat food, will die. But it doesn't just take the simple act of reading to be strong in our walk. I must challenge myself to find what I believe to be true and choose to live by those convictions, relying on Jesus for my strength.

I've been a Christian for almost fifteen years. There have been ups and downs in my life. In this time, I've learned many things the hard way. I've made both huge and minor mistakes. I've learned it doesn't just take reading the truth; it takes applying it to my life. It takes choosing truth. It takes meditating on the truth. It takes sitting down and asking, "What do I believe and want my life to say about me? Where do I stand? When asked, will I have an answer for the hope that is in me (1 Peter 3:15)? Can I defend my faith?" And when I've figured out what I believe, it's important that I've asked myself if my life reflects those things. I have strong opinions about a lot of things, but am I living in such a way that backs up those stances? If I'm not, I'm the definition of a hypocrite. Which I am. I will never perfectly practice what I preach. But before I open my mouth to tell the world what I stand for, maybe I should just simply stand for it, showing with my life what I believe. If I'm living what I'm speaking, I won't have to speak nearly as much.

> Beloved, I beg *you* as sojourners and pilgrims, abstain from fleshly lusts which war against the soul, having your conduct honorable among the Gentiles, that

when they speak against you as evildoers, they may, by *your* good works which they observe, glorify God in the day of visitation. (1 Peter 2:11–12)

PRAYER

Lord, please fill me up to overflowing. I want to be bursting at the seams with Your love.

....

....

....

....

....

....

....

....

....

....

....

....

continue your personal prayer

WHAT SIDE WOULD YOU BE ON?

Lately, while studying the Gospels, a question has been coming to mind. What side would you be on if you were back in Jesus's time? This question humbles me, although I wish I could answer honestly that I would most definitely be like Mary, worshiping at Jesus's feet; most times, I don't believe that would be the case. I'd most likely be the one saying, "Who do You think you are? You think You can just walk in here and tell us what to do? What makes You any better than us?"

I can be so critical of the Jewish leaders. I can pass so much judgment on their hard hearts and blinded minds. I can say, "How could they do that to Jesus?" but we have the whole book. We see how it ends. We see how everything in the Old Testament points to Jesus, points to this moment in time when Jesus comes on the scene. In all actuality, if I'm honest with myself, I can't pass judgment on them. I am them. How often in my life have I metaphorically said, "I will not have this man rule over me, over my life"? I'm the one who nailed Him to the cross. I'm the one who needs His forgiveness every day. I'm a sinner who is so, so thankful for His love and forgiveness.

> There is none righteous, no, not one; there is none who understands; none who seeks after God. (Romans 3:10–11)

PRAYER

Lord, thank You! You didn't have to die for us, but You did. You love us so much, and I couldn't be any more thankful. Continue to reveal Yourself to my heart.

....

....

....

....

....

....

....

....

....

....

....

....

continue your personal prayer

REDEEMED

Sometimes I get frustrated with myself. "Why am I still dealing with this? Why is this popping up again? I thought I was over it."

The truth of the matter is I will have good days and bad days, but shame, regret, and the past are things I will constantly and continually have to give back to God, remembering that He has redeemed me. He no longer sees those things; they're gone! We as humans can't understand this kind of forgiveness, because we can forgive, but we don't easily forget. With Jesus, it is different. The second I ask for forgiveness, it's done. It's forgotten. It's at the ocean's floor.

I will struggle with the past at times. I will struggle with forgiving myself. Sometimes remembering that He has washed me clean is the only thing strengthening me to walk in the authority He alone has given me. The authority of new life. The authority to speak truth of the pain we will experience when we don't do it His way. And also the truth of redemption. I can say with absolute certainty that if He can forgive and redeem me, He can forgive and redeem you. I've experienced it. I've lived it!

> In Him we have redemption through His blood, the forgiveness of sins, according to the riches of His grace which He made to abound toward us in all wisdom and prudence, having made known to us the mystery of His will, according to His good pleasure which He purposed in Himself, that in the dispensation of the fullness of the times He might gather together in one all things in Christ, both which are in heaven and which are on earth—in Him. (Ephesians 1:7–10)

PRAYER

Lord, please clear out all the lies that tell me I am beyond redemption. You are the God who redeems. Your angels sing praises when one sinner repents! Thank You for Your forgiveness that is beyond anything we can comprehend. Let us be more like You in forgiving others.

continue your personal prayer

HE WANTS
MY HEART

I talk about distractions a lot, but it's because they are everywhere. Everywhere we turn, there is something demanding our attention. Whether it's work, family, friends, or my desires, it can be so easy to get caught up in things of this life and forget the things of Jesus.

Here, lately, I have been struggling. I sit down in the mornings to do my quiet time, and my mind is all over the place. I can't focus on what God is trying to speak to me. I get frustrated with myself feeling, as if I'm failing Him. Something I felt Him impress upon my heart today is this: "Baylee, you're treating our relationship like a job or a duty. I want your love, and I want you to enjoy spending time with Me." This is the reality of it. I love Jesus, but there are times when I treat my time with Him as a duty. What if I treated my husband or people I love this way, like spending time with them was just something to check off the to-do list? Sit down, look at my watch, and say, "Well, I've got thirty minutes; you need to hurry and speak to me. Then I'll tell you what I need from you, and we'll wrap this up until tomorrow." That would be an insane way to treat my friends and loved ones.

When I start to feel this way, when I feel like I'm doing my Bible reading out of a sense of duty, I need to remind myself of His love and desire for my heart, not just my time. My time means absolutely nothing to Him if I'm sitting down to check a box and if it's a chore on the list.

Jesus said to him, "'You shall love the Lord your God with all your heart, with all your soul, and with all your mind.' This is *the* first and great commandment." (Matthew 22:37–38)

PRAYER

Lord, have my heart. I know I'm too sinful to fully, willfully give it to you, so I pray You will take it. Use my heart and my life to further Your kingdom.

....

....

....

....

....

....

....

....

....

....

....

continue your personal prayer

STRIVE FOR LOVE

Where love is present, sin is not. Our world has gotten that word *love* twisted and distorted. But in most cases, in our world, the word *love* can be something selfish. True love serves. True love does what is best for others. And in true love, the entire law is fulfilled. If you truly love God, you won't serve any other gods. If you truly love God, you won't have idols. A common saying in our society is "Love yourself, or you won't be able to love others." Jesus says, "Deny yourself, take up your cross, and follow Me." Society is telling us to be selfish, to always put ourselves first, while Jesus tells us to be *selfless* and esteem others higher than ourselves.

If you truly love God, you won't use His name in vain. You will rest in Him. If you truly love God, you will honor your father and mother. If you have true love, you won't murder. You will not commit adultery. If you have true love, you won't steal. If you have true love, you will not lie. If you love, you will not want what other people have.

By the way, it's impossible! These are all part of the law of the Old Testament; humanity failed to follow all these rules all the time.

We do not have perfect love; this is why Jesus died for us. But instead of striving to keep the law or be a better person, we should strive to have true and more perfect love. Because the whole law can be completed if we love (Galatians 5:14).

PRAYER

Lord, let us increase in love one for another. Let love overflow from Your Holy Spirit within us.

DRINK WATER

The Word is like water. The things of this world are like caffeine. Caffeine gives you energy quickly, until you crash an hour later. Then you need more, which is just dehydrating you more, zapping more of the water from your system, which makes you more tired. When we drink water, however, we are hydrating and have energy that lasts. When we have headaches or caffeine cravings, our bodies are actually craving water. But if we drink caffeine, our headaches go away, so we drink coffee instead. But if we drink enough caffeine, our body starts to need it the way it needed water. Have you ever tried to quit caffeine? I have a few different times in life. It takes weeks of headaches and tiredness to break the caffeine habit and get back to just water.

The same is true in our spiritual lives. We start out with the water. We have a lot of energy, and then we drink a little coffee, a little bit of what the world has to offer. This hit gives us a little more energy, and it feels really good for a while. Then we crash, so we drink a little more and a little more. Pretty soon, we are so dehydrated for the true, refreshing water of the Word of God and feeling sick. We decide to cut back on the caffeine, but then we have to deal with the headaches and exhaustion that come with it.

When I start indulging in worldly entertainment, I enjoy it at first, much like the coffee. It's funny or exciting; it gives an energy boost at first. But long-term, it drains me of the true, abundant life that God promises those who abide in Him. But it's hard to quit indulging in the world once we've started. It's better to just not start. Moral of the story … drink the water. Fill up on the water of the Word! Drink deep in Jesus!

PRAYER

Lord, increase my desire for Your living water. Let the things of this world not be attractive to me, knowing they're empty; let them fade into the background.

....

....

....

....

....

....

....

....

....

....

....

....

....

continue your personal prayer

WHAT
IS TRUTH?

Our world says, "There is so no such thing as absolute truth." But that statement contradicts itself. If there is no truth, then that very statement can't be made in truth. In order to say, "There is no truth," you are saying, "My statement about no truth is true."

The reality is there has to be such a thing as truth. Ask anyone if there is such a thing as absolute truth. If they say no, ask if it is wrong to murder. Most likely, they would say it is wrong. If they said it wasn't wrong to murder, first of all, you should probably run away. That person might be a psycho. But if you're brave, just ask them if they think it would be all right for them to be murdered.

Ask if it's wrong to steal. If they say no, then ask if you can steal from them. With these questions, eventually you will get a no answer. Then just ask if that no answer is true. If all things really are relative, then if it benefits me to steal from you, or to kill, what's the problem? We are all just accidents anyway, right? But reality is our moral code—right and wrong—is written deep within our being. Innately, we know there is absolute truth, whether we choose to deny it or not. That's what's relative.

After Jesus said, "I have come to bear witness of the truth," Pilate said to Him, "What is truth?" (John 18:38a).

What is truth? This question is so important. This question demands an answer. We must take the time to find for ourselves absolute truth. It's important in our current political climate that we are convinced for ourselves what truth is. Spoiler alert, it's Jesus! He's the way, the truth, and the life!

PRAYER

Lord, reveal absolute truth to my heart. Let me know You deeply.

....

....

....

....

....

....

....

....

....

....

....

continue your personal prayer

THIS LIFE

These things I have spoken to you, that in Me you may
have peace. In the world you will have tribulation; but
be of good cheer, I have overcome the world.
—John 16:33

You will have trouble in this life. It won't always be smooth sailing. It's funny because lately I've been struggling to be in intimacy with Jesus. In Mexico, it was so much easier to focus on what was important because my whole day and whole life there was completely focused on pouring into myself with the intentional purpose of pouring out to others. When I first came home, this was still my focus, but it's amazing how quickly water can become stagnant without an outlet. Pouring out is the only way to stay fresh and healthy in our walk with Jesus. And although there are so many opportunities in my daily life, I find myself distracted by the things I need to get done in a day. I need to slow down, take a deep breath, and look for the hurts around me that give me the chance to lift someone up. Life is too short to waste the time I'm given to change my little part of the world. In focusing on furthering His kingdom, God will be glorified with my life. I will store up for myself treasures in heaven. I will be blessed and refreshed with the inpouring and outpouring of fresh water, and I will be a blessing to those around me. What greater abundant life is there than simply doing Jesus's will?

PRAYER

Lord, let abundant life flow through me to others. Let me be a vessel to bring fresh water to the hurting around me. Lord, use my life.

....

....

....

....

....

....

....

....

....

....

....

....

....

continue your personal prayer

DO YOU LOVE ME?

Jesus asked Peter three times if he loved Him, the same number that, on the day Jesus was betrayed, Peter denied he ever knew Him.

In Greek, there are a six different words for love, but there are two different words used here in John, chapter 21, philia and agape. Philia is a friendship love, and agape is the most radical love; it means love unconditional, without end.

Jesus, in this chapter, asks Peter the first two times, "Peter do you love (agape) Me?"

To which Peter replies, "Lord, I love (phileo) You."

To put this in English terms, Jesus asks, "Do you love Me?" and Peter replies, "I really like You."

The third time, Jesus asks, "Peter, do you love (phileo) Me?"

Okay, Peter, "Do you even like me?"

It says his heart was broken, and Peter replies, "Lord, I love (agape) You."

I believe this is the moment when Peter realizes, "No, I don't love You the way I need to." This is the moment when Peter makes the choice to truly love (agape) Jesus.

This made me ask myself, "Baylee, do you love Jesus?" Do I love Him unconditionally and without end? Or is He just my buddy who does things for me? My genie in a bottle who grants me wishes. Will the circumstances of life, the struggles, change how I love Him? It's important to test myself on this. I want to agape love Him, to where if He's all that I have left, He's all that I need.

After each time Jesus asks and Peter says, "Yes, I love You." Jesus says, "Feed my lambs." "Tend my sheep." "Feed my sheep."

The way that I show my love is by serving God's people and those around me.

PRAYER

Lord, test my heart. Let me love You with all of me!

....

....

....

....

....

....

....

....

....

....

....

....

continue your personal prayer

ARMOR OF GOD

Soldiers look like civilians until they put on the uniform; they blend in with the rest of the world. Once they put on the uniform and carry a gun, they are now a target for the enemy. Once they are recognized as soldiers, they must always be wearing the armor because they are a target, and an even bigger target when they are vulnerable without their armor. The marines have a rule of no soldier left behind, which the enemy can take advantage of. If they can just wound an unprotected soldier, then two or three have to stop fighting to tend to that one soldier. If you have enough wounded, you have a pretty debilitated army.

Our enemy, the enemy of our souls, uses this tactic as well. I must make sure that I keep fighting, not that I don't stop to take care of hurting brothers and sisters, but I must make sure that I am wearing all my armor and am living in protection through the life of Jesus.

My whole life, I've heard this saying of "put on the armor of God." I've heard it taught in Sunday school, and I've seen the *Veggie Tales* episode, but what does that actually mean or look like in real life terms? Well, let's take a look.

Here is my interpretation of the armor of God in Ephesians 6:10–20 ... hopefully in practical terms: putting on the belt of truth (knowing what I believe to be true and searching that out in the scriptures for myself); wearing my breastplate, or bulletproof vest, of righteousness (righteousness means very good or excellent, to know that God has made me very good and excellent is to walk with integrity and confidence, not crippled by shame but knowing who I am as the bride of Christ, knowing what He's done for me; this is my protection against the death blows of the enemy); feet shod with the preparation of the gospel of peace (pouring out the peace of Jesus is what is going to keep me moving and give me energy to keep fighting the good fight). I must take up my shield of faith. (Faith is my biggest protection. Having faith that God always has a plan in everything that happens in life is protection during the battles of life.). I need to put on my helmet of salvation. (I need my head, and the helmet protects the head. Without salvation, there is no eternal life, just like without the head, there is no life.). I need to take up the sword of the spirit, which is the Word of God. (This is not my sword. It's the spirit's. Far too often, I see people using the Gospel as their weapon and hurting people with it. The Gospel, which is a double-edged sword, is always to be directed by the spirit.)

I must be sure I am protecting myself in Jesus first, with all my armor on, because if I get wounded for lack of protection, I'm not only debilitating myself from the fight, but I am also putting my fellow soldiers at risk as well.

> Be on your guard; stand firm in the faith; be courageous; be strong. Do everything in love. (1 Corinthians 16:13)

PRAYER

Lord, thank You for Your armor and protection! You are such a good Father. Give us grace for the fight of this life.

....

....

....

....

continue your personal prayer

ABOVE THE NOISE

Be still and know that I am God ...
—Psalm 46:10a

Lately, I have had a real problem with quietly sitting and listening to Jesus. I always have to be doing something, listening to something, or reading something.

In Mexico, I was not supposed to go off by myself. Mexico is kind of dangerous for young girls. I'm not the best at following rules. I'm also an introvert in nature, and with how wild, loud, and obnoxious our city was, and rooming with eight other girls on our base, I frequently ran up to the lighthouse to get some quiet. It was about three miles outside of the city, and I can't tell you how peaceful it was. God not only blessed me with protection (I was kind of a silly, naïve girl), but He also blessed me with so much more. How big of a blessing it is to be above clouds and the noise, to only see water for miles and miles and realize just how big and creative our God is. This was my favorite place ... possibly my favorite place on earth. There aren't any words for the number of fond memories I have for this particular place and the ways God met me there.

Since coming home, since becoming a wife and a mom, I haven't found a lighthouse—a place to be above the noise. But the Lord is revealing to me it's not the physical location; it's the heart location. The reason I was able to meet with Him was because my heart was listening. That is the key. Most of the time, the real obnoxious noise is in my head. My mind can be a very wild place, a place of pain, a place of fear, a place of shame and regret. Those thoughts can be so loud in there that they overpower the voice of Jesus and obliterate His peace. Being still in His presence allows Him to speak to my heart and minister to my soul, restoring peace and recuperating my mind. When we truly encounter the living, loving God, we can't help but praise and serve Him. It's important to remember, in life, as we go through mountains and valleys, no matter where we are, God is right there waiting for us to look to Him. You simply have to be still and listen. He has a quiet, peaceful voice that we can't hear unless our hearts are above the noise.

PRAYER

Lord, let my heart hear You today. Please help me quiet the chaos within my soul and listen for Your still, small voice, the only voice bringing peace to my life.

....

....

....

....

....

....

....

....

continue your personal prayer

IF I'M NOT LIVING IT, IS IT EVEN TRUE?

We were created to be worshippers. We were created to be devoted to someone. Everyone in one way or another worships and is devoted to something. The question is, what?

> There is none righteous, no, not one; There is none who understands; There is none who seeks after God. (Romans 3:10–11)

I know that there is nothing good in me, but through the grace and love of Jesus and His transformation of my life, I can truly say, in my heart, all I want in life is to love and worship Jesus with all my heart and to glorify Him with my life.

But, being the fickle human I am, is this how I go about my day? If I'm not living it, is what I say even true? If the enemy can't cause me to turn away from God, he will try any and everything to make me ineffective in my world. I can say all these things, but then I must go and do them. I must fight the enemy's words when he says, "Who are you? You can't change anything." The reality is I have the only thing that can change my world, hope in Jesus. The enemy knows this fact, which is why he tries so hard to make me keep it to myself. If I'm in the limbo of saying something but not living it, the enemy can have a foothold, which he can use to make me ineffective in my life. I'm the safest and most effective when everyone knows I'm sold out to Jesus. I'm in the worst danger when I'm surrounded by people who don't know I'm a Christian. It's so much easier to compromise here and there, and before I know it, Satan is in my ear saying. "You just said that off-colored joke. You better not let them know you're a Christian now."

> "I know your works, that you are neither cold nor hot. I could wish you were cold or hot. So then, because you are lukewarm, and neither cold nor hot, I will vomit you out of My mouth." (Revelation 3:15–16)

We must make a decision. We must be hot for Jesus. The most dangerous place is lukewarm. We're not promised tomorrow. I don't want to waste today building my kingdom here when I will spend eternity elsewhere. I'd like to take as many souls with me as I can.

> Therefore submit to God. Resist the devil and he will flee from you. (James 4:7)

PRAYER

Lord, let us not be lukewarm Christians. Let us be sold out for You in every way, in every fiber of our being.

....

....

....

....

....

continue your personal prayer

"I AM STILL GROWING YOU"

Lately, I've been believing this lie, that I'm not growing anymore. It's because in Mexico I was spending six to ten hours a day in Bible study, worship, prayer, or serving people. Coming home, I feel like I'm failing or like God is disappointed in me because I'm not doing the same thing. I put expectations on myself and listen to a voice that is not God saying, "You need to do more." I get irritated, disappointed, and fearful with myself when I don't meet my expectations. I'm scared to death of walking away from my Savior, because I know from experience I'm not safe in this world alone. I also know how prone I am to wander.

I should strive for perfection daily. I should always miss my mark because I am always aiming to be like Jesus. But I must remember God is not disappointed or irritated when I fail or fall. He has no expectations of us because he knows we will fail. That's why He sent Jesus to die in our place. When He looks at us, He sees perfection. He sees Jesus.

He reminded me this morning, "Either you're walking forward toward Me, or you're walking backward away from Me. There is no middle ground. But, Baylee, if you are striving every day to deepen your relationship with Me, you are walking forward. I'm still growing you. Do not be anxious. Do not be afraid."

It is foolish for me to think that meeting with the creator every day wouldn't grow or change me. He does the work in and through me. Doing more isn't what it's about. I am to seek Him and to be obedient to what He calls me to do, and that is all. If I try to do things on my own, I'm sure to mess it up. I'm only called to experience Him and tell others what I've witnessed. That is all. But to be a witness of Him, I have to first experience Him and His goodness.

> But when they deliver you up, do not worry about how or what you should speak. For it will be given to you in that hour what you should speak; for it is not you who speak, but the Spirit of your Father who speaks in you. (Mathew 10:20)

PRAYER

Lord, let me rest in Your promises. You know my fears of ending up far from You. I'm afraid of my own sin nature. Protect me. Hold me close, the way only You can.

....

....

....

....

....

....

....

....

continue your personal prayer

A COUNTERFEIT,
A FRAUD

A counterfeit has to be close enough to the true thing to be passed off *as* the true thing. I once watched this show on TV about an ex-convict showing how he used to make counterfeit money (they left out a key step, so no, I unfortunately can't replicate it). He said they used to take real five-dollar bills, wash all the ink off with a certain kind of chemical, and then print them into fifty-dollar bills, or take ten-dollar bills and print them into hundred-dollar bills. This way, the money would feel the same, and at one glance, at the counterfeit control bar when you held it to the light, it would look like the real thing. Only if you studied it would you realize it was a fraud.

Satan is a counterfeit. Sometimes he attacks me in such a complex way that it seems like conviction. It's not until I truly sit down to pray about a matter that I realize it's not God's voice.

The way I test this is to study the thoughts or feelings that I have against the Bible, namely Jesus's character. Even when I see Jesus correct someone harshly, it is always from a gentle place and brings peace to the children of God. I ask myself, "Is this conviction bringing peace or fear? Is what I seem to be convicted of coming from reason or fear?" God says 365 times, "Do not be afraid." If we find ourselves fearful from this so-called conviction, or fear is the reason for the so-called conviction, we can be 100 percent certain it is not from God. Satan's counterfeit can feel exactly like conviction, except with too much fear, like a recipe that's exactly the same but with too much salt. Something's just not right.

I'll give an example of this in my life. When I was looking to go to Mexico, I was praying about it, trying to make sure it was God's plan for me. At one point, I got this overwhelming fear come over me. It felt like conviction, like God was saying, "Don't go. This is not My plan." But the more I prayed about it, and the more God provided the money and the means to go, and after seeing the incredible blessing it was in my life, I realize that was an extreme attack from the enemy not wanting me to go. But he disguised his voice and the feeling of my heart to look like a conviction from God. Satan wants us running from God. He wants us afraid because when we mess up, and certainly we will, he wants our first reaction to be to run away in shame.

I must bring confusing situations to God, the counterfeit expert, study it with Him, and allow Him to teach me; otherwise, I may glance at it and pass it off as the real thing.

> Be sober, be vigilant; because your adversary the devil walks about like a roaring lion, seeking whom he may devour. (1 Peter 5:8)

PRAYER

Lord, let my motivation be to honor You. When I mess up, let me run to You in repentance. Let me be wise to the enemy's counterfeits. Let me not believe his lies.

....

....

....

....

continue your personal prayer

JESUS'S FEET
DON'T STINK

We were created to worship. We will worship eternally at the feet of Jesus in heaven. To some and to me, that sometimes doesn't sound so enjoyable. Like, really? That's all we'll do?

Now worship isn't just singing. Worship is a state of heart. It's a heart of thanks and an intimate desire to be close to God. It isn't until I get into a true heart of worship that I realize that's all I want to do. I find I am the most miserable when I step outside of worship, and I am the most joyful and at peace the more I worship. The more I spend time with my creator, the more I desire to be with Him. The problem is, for some reason, in my life, I forget. I forget that the best place to be, the only satisfying place to be, is at the feet of Jesus, my Savior. Sometimes I forget there is no such thing as too much worship, too much time spent with Him. But I notice if I step outside of that state of worship, I start to look to other things to satisfy me and realize that everything is vanity and greatly disappointing. More money, more things, more entertainment just produces hunger for more. Stuff is not a satisfying god, but stuff can become a god too easily. We think idolatry doesn't exist today? Think again. An idol is anything I desire more than God Himself. Not that stuff is a bad thing in and of itself, but I must be careful to not put anything before God.

More of Jesus, in the same way, produces a hunger for more of Him. The difference is the hunger for Him never disappoints. It's the definition of fullness of life. To run after Jesus with my whole heart is the only place I will find life.

And this is eternal life, that they may know You, the only true God, and Jesus Christ whom You have sent. (John 17:3)

PRAYER

Lord, cause me to come to You. Cause me to drink deeply of Your living water that truly gives me life.

....

....

....

....

....

....

....

....

....

....

....

....

continue your personal prayer

BE OBEDIENT

When I was first told to write a book, there were so many doubts and fears that came to mind.

You're not good enough. Who'd want to read what you write anyway? What if it fails? There are so many people who are going to judge you. You can't be honest about your struggles; you can't be honest about your past. Hardly anyone outside your family knows your true story. You can't share it publicly.

Okay. That's it. I'm not going to do it. It's too hard. No one would want to read it. It would be a waste of my time anyway, I thought as I closed my Bible to get ready for church.

It just so happened that that the entire message that Sunday was about being obedient to God. Not needing to understand what He is doing, simply taking the next step in faith that is opened up ahead of you. "Are you goanna do what I want you to and allow Me to further redeem your life for My glory and your good? It's your choice. I can find someone else."

Conviction came over me as He spoke this to my heart. How many times have I prayed to be used by Him, but in reality, I want Him to use me only in the comfortable, fun ways. "Okay, Lord, point taken." I went straight home and started writing.

This book has been a labor of love for eight years. In that time, I've grown in my relationship with Jesus, gotten married, had three children, and fought through many spiritual battles to complete this project.

Being given this vision, this dream, so many years ago, I didn't realize until I was in the process of editing these devotionals that the Lord had so much more He needed me to learn to actually make this dream a reality. From knowledge to wisdom to life experience, to simple writing skills and style, I needed to practice a lot in life to be ready for this challenge.

Whatever He lays on your heart to do, no matter the fears you might have, just start doing it. You'll be amazed at how He grows you through the process!

> Then Jesus said to His disciples, "If anyone desires to come after Me, let him deny himself, and take up his cross, and follow Me. For whoever desires to save his life will lose it, but whoever loses his life for My sake will find it." (Matthew 16:24–25)

PRAYER

Lord, let me live fearless and humbly within Your will for my life.

....

....

....

....

....

....

....

....

continue your personal prayer

I WANT LIFE TO THE FULLEST. WHO'S WITH ME?

How miserable life can be when I am just living on repeat, forgetting who I'm supposed to be living for. Work, eat, sleep, repeat. Even a simple conversation with a friend talking about Jesus our Lord can make all the difference in a day. Pouring out can become an addiction. Spreading God's love and hope can be the most fun and fulfilling thing I do in a day. Oh, how quickly I forget that feeling, the fullness of serving God and His people. I turn to things of the world to satisfy that longing and always come up short. It isn't until a simple question asked by my boss gives me the chance to answer with truth, a simple conversation with a friend reminding me of the faithfulness of God, or the blessing of a relationship completely devoted to growing in His ways that I realize just how truly fulfilling the joy of speaking His name is. If I could just keep that in the forefront of my brain and the goal of my heart each and every day, how much more of a joyful blessing I would be to my world.

> As you therefore have received Christ Jesus the Lord, so walk in Him, rooted and built up in Him and established in the faith, as you have been taught, abounding in it with thanksgiving.

Beware lest anyone cheat you through philosophy and empty deceit, according to the tradition of men, according to the basic principles of the world, and not according to Christ. (Colossians 2:6–8)

PRAYER

Lord, I love You. I want fullness of life. Let me be a stream of fresh water, always pouring in so that I can pour out.

....

....

....

....

....

....

....

....

....

....

....

continue your personal prayer

I CAN HANDLE IT

Our world puts ratings of maturity on entertainment. I think this is one of the biggest deceits of the enemy in the lives of Christians.

The more we engage in content only suitable for mature people, whether it be violence, foul language, sex, or whatever, the more we get desensitized to the evil things of this world.

The world says that, as a child, you should focus on, as Philippians 4:8 says, whatever is right, whatever is pure, whatever is lovely; if anything is excellent or praiseworthy, think about such things. Why do we want our children to watch these things? Because we want them to hang onto their innocence. We want their minds to be pure and lovely and for them to live life without fear or heartache. But when they turn thirteen, we say okay, now we can start revealing to them the more perverted things. They can start to see movies that are a little more racy. We'll slowly fade them into the reality of life. What a lie. Why don't we want our kids to grow up and be pure, innocent, lovely, godly adults? What's wrong with that? It's because our world is cruel. Our world tells us, "As they grow up, kids need to know pain. They need to understand the evil around us. They need to know this world is not all purple ponies and rainbows." Our world even makes fun of virgins and innocent adult characters in movies. You know why they make fun of it? Because they want it. Talk to anyone who has engaged in such activities seen in even a PG-13 movie. I guarantee they will either call those things mistakes, or they will lie. God commands us to be wise as serpents but innocent as doves (Matthew 10:16). Wisdom and innocence come from being filled with the Holy Spirit and being washed in the water from His

Word, the Gospel, continually. You can always be cleansed from your actions. You can always repent from watching filth, but those images stay in your brain forever. The biggest lie from Satan in the Christian life is "You can handle it." Everything that we take in is what will flow out. Be sure what you're taking in is what you want to pour out.

PRAYER

Lord, give me a desire for innocence and purity. Let me love the things of You.

....

....

....

....

....

....

....

....

....

....

continue your personal prayer

SHORT AND SWEET BUT A GOOD REMINDER

The enemy is after our souls. It is so important for us to remember that if our focus is to serve God with our lives, Satan is threatened. He will try to make things as hard as he possibly can. He may attack in ways unrelated to the way we are serving, but make no mistake, the moment we decide to live for Jesus is the very moment Satan will do his very best to make us stop. He may attack in relationships, financially, with health problems, or with temptation. The account of Job shows us some of the difficulties Satan can use against us in our lives, and like Job, Satan's whole objective first and foremost is to get us to turn our backs on the Lord. If he can't accomplish this, he would be happy to at the very least have us sin and hurt others and ourselves. He will attack us where we're weakest, and there's never a time when we're safe on our own. Finding our strength in Jesus is the only way we will be able to stand up to the blows and continue to fight the good fight.

> "These things I have spoken to you, that in Me you may have peace. In the world you will have tribulation; but be of good cheer, I have overcome the world." (John 16:32)

PRAYER

Lord, let Your love be my hiding place. In You I find the refuge my soul needs. Let my love for You be without fear, for You have overcome the world.

....

....

....

....

....

....

....

....

....

....

....

....

....

continue your personal prayer

REMIND MYSELF OF
HIS GREATNESS

Sometimes I listen to a song, or get caught out in a thunderstorm, or see the magnificent beauty of a sunrise, which a camera cannot even begin to capture. It's in those moments I'm reminded of the incredible creativity and power of our God. A power we can so easily forget. A God who dusts the darkness with sparkles at night and paints the sky with a new shade of brilliant light every morning. A God who created palm trees that can withstand the strongest of hurricane winds, a God who commands the lightning bolts. Yes, the raw power of our God should amaze us.

Even more than that, His love should overwhelm us. The God who has all the creation of the world to worship Him created me and desires my heart! Why? How? Such an unfaithful heart like mine? So prone to wonder from Him, why would He desire me? The more I walk with Jesus, the more convinced I am that I can do nothing good for Him! Anything good that can be done in me is done by Him and His power anyway! That's not something that my brain can even begin to comprehend. But how quickly, if I'm not careful, can that awe of His love wear off. I have to continually remind myself of His greatness and remind my heart to choose Him.

> For since the creation of the world His invisible
> *attributes* are clearly seen, being understood by the
> things that are made, *even* His eternal power and
> Godhead, so that they are without excuse, because,
> although they knew God, they did not glorify *Him*

as God, nor were thankful, but became futile in their thoughts, and their foolish hearts were darkened. Professing to be wise, they became fools, and changed the glory of the incorruptible God into an image made like corruptible man—and birds and four-footed animals and creeping things. (Romans 1:20–23)

PRAYER

Lord, let me contemplate Your love. Let me be overcome by Your grace for me.

....

....

....

....

....

....

....

....

....

....

continue your personal prayer

WHAT DOES MY LIFE SAY ABOUT ME?

I tend to be a quiet, introverted person by nature, but my spirit longs for every person who ever meets me to see the light of Jesus in me. Sometimes my flesh and awkward personality get in the way of that. Sometimes I catch myself wanting them to see Jesus for the sheer purpose of people liking me, which isn't the correct heart posture to be used by Him. My hope and prayers are that I can preach the character of God with my life. I want to make a difference in my sphere of influence with the only true light and the only hope for this world. I don't want to get caught up in having a big name for myself, or even a small, very liked name. I want to be caught up in the name of Jesus and making His name known.

In Acts 14:8, Paul healed a crippled man. The multitudes of people started worshiping Barnabas and Paul as gods. A few verses later (14:19), in a rapid plot twist, they stone Paul, thinking and hoping they killed him, and they drag him out of the city.

Don't live life to please people. One minute, they might be singing your praises, and the next, they hate you more than anything. Live to please Jesus, who is the same yesterday, today, and forever, in whom all blessing are sure. The rewards stored for you in heaven are better than any praises, likes, or fame here on earth, and those rewards never pass away.

People are so fickle; they can change their mind in an instant. If I'm living for the applause of men, I'm sure to be shattered when the stoning comes. I would rather be living to please Jesus, who never changes.

Sometimes I wonder how well I'm doing at this mission He has placed in my heart. If I wasn't such a selfish sinner, I'd be able to do such a better job at spreading His Word, but I guess if I wasn't such a sinner, maybe Jesus wouldn't have had to come in the first place. Bottom line, I think it's best to be in a humble place of realizing our sins and shortcomings, agreeing with our adversary when he calls us worthless. I am worthless without Jesus dwelling in me, but He gives me the power to move mountains. He gives me the power to overcome sin and addiction. He gives me the power to live life entirely for Him.

PRAYER

Lord, I want to be unashamed of the Gospel and the hope it brings to our world. Give me the passion I need for Your Word and the courage I need to live entirely for You.

....

....

....

....

....

....

....

continue your personal prayer

I WANT TO DO HUGE THINGS FOR HIM

I want to do something world changing like the disciples in the Bible who were martyred in order to further the Gospel, or William Tyndale facing death for printing the Bible in English, or Martin Luther King Jr., who stood for human rights.

It's so easy to get caught up in doing something monumental that we miss the chance to do something small, something that will bless just one person.

I understand that God will leave the one thousand to go after the one, so I need to be willing to speak to that one who God puts in my path. He can and will use us mightily if we give Him the chance, but we must not underestimate the effect in heaven when just one soul gets saved. Instead of focusing on quantity, I should be focused on the one person put in my path to talk to today. I want to dream about the ripple effect of one life changed. We all know the name Billy Graham. Do we know who brought Billy Graham to the Lord? Or the person who brought that person to the Lord? We don't need a huge-scale platform to make a huge-scale difference. We must just be obedient. Jesus does all the work anyhow. How many lives could be affected from just one changed life? Never underestimate the effect you could make on this world by simply being obedient to what He tells you to do. Ask Him to use you. Ask Him for the courage. Never waste a chance to speak into someone's life.

And the world is passing away, and the lust of it; but he who does the will of God abides forever. (1 John 2:17)

PRAYER

Lord, let me simply be obedient to You. Let me listen to Your voice. Use me and give me courage to be obedient.

....

....

....

....

....

....

....

....

....

....

....

continue your personal prayer

WATCHING THE SUNRISE

I love sunrises.

No matter how many I see, I'm filled with awe every single morning.

How could a God who creates so much beauty every morning ever think of me? I can be such a dirty, rotten sinner. I rejected and nailed Him to the cross! His amazing love and mercy I will never understand. A question I will ask for all eternity is "How can it be?"

He loves me? For no other reason than He wants to love me? I can't comprehend that love!

In our fallen state of being, humans love mostly with conditions. Only through Jesus can we begin to understand sacrificial love, but even most Christians have a hard time loving this way. If I was in an unfaithful marriage, where that person brought nothing to the table, did nothing for me, and hardly listened to any of my desires, it would be very difficult to love that person. However, this is the exact relationship in which Jesus chose and chooses us. For while we were yet sinners, Christ died for us (Romans 5:8). He chose us before we ever turned to Him. He chose us while we were still unfaithful, still rebellious, not desiring righteousness. We can rest knowing that because He chose us in our unrighteousness, there is nothing we can do to earn His love. He loves us because He chose to love us. His love is completely unconditional. Rest in this today.

PRAYER

Lord, let me realize Your complete and radical love. Let this change my heart. Let me be in submission to You because of this profound love. Let my heart, though prone to do evil, be faithful to You out of love.

....

....

....

....

....

....

....

....

....

....

....

....

continue your personal prayer

HOW DOES IT GO?

(I wrote this devotional on my blog almost seven years ago, the morning after being engaged to my now husband. I got married almost exactly one year after getting out of one of the most difficult times and relationships of my life—one year after a time in life where suicide was never far from my thoughts and life itself felt hopeless, empty, and dark. The prior year was filled with intense healing, and in the moment of writing this, I was absolutely in awe of my creator, the redemption He had brought to my life, the protection He provided through my many mistakes. It was beyond my comprehension.)

This morning has been one of bafflement, pure excitement and wonder! I serve an awesome God! He has blessed me with an incredible family, great friends, and an amazing husband and family to be!

Every time I think about my redeemer, I'm just filled with awe of how much grace He has extended to me in my life! This beautiful story of the mess that I was, being blessed and cherished for no other reason than He loves me and wants to bless me! Why would He want to bless me? I have done nothing for Him! I have made a mess of His name and my name. But He still loves me unconditionally! This is the love that I can't comprehend and the love that I want to have toward every person in my life! The grace and mercy I have been shown, I must extend to others. With this unconditional love I have been shown, I must fiercely love others. I am truly blessed beyond belief.

If you don't know my God, you need to meet Him. He's

incredible! If you do, take a moment to be mesmerized by His greatness today. In this busy world, it's easy to forget, but take a moment to remember what He's done for you.

> For by grace you have been saved through faith, and that not of yourselves; *it is* the gift of God, not of works, lest anyone should boast. (Ephesians 2:8–9)

PRAYER

Lord, thank You for Your wonderful blessings, for choosing me no matter what mistakes I've made. Thank You for being the God who redeems. Remind me of Your greatness right now.

continue your personal prayer

TIMES OF OVERWHELMING BLESSING

(Again, I wrote this while planning my wedding which was to take place in four weeks.)

I know every soon-to-be bride has excitement beyond belief. I'm not going to pretend my excitement is unique in that way. What I will say is that my excitement comes from my overwhelmingly forgiving God! It wasn't too long ago that God picked me up out of the pit I had found myself in. It wasn't too long ago that, for the first time, I experienced His eternal forgiveness, His unfailing, steadfast love.

There were so many experiences of God's profound love running after me. I honestly showed up in Mexico believing in the deepest part of my heart that I wouldn't ever be fully forgiven. When I got to my room, sitting on my bed was a letter written to me anonymously by a complete stranger who had been praying for me. No one knew my story, but God gave this person a prophetic vision to share with me; they saw a sweet little cottage in the middle of the woods, with a garden and a picket fence around it. It was beautiful and sweet. But the gate got left open for Satan, and he was slowly entering the house, destroying everything within the fence. This person's message to me was to lock Satan out.

Week four, while in class, we were told to find a quiet place and draw a picture. I believe I got this picture from the Lord. I was down in the bottom of this huge tower, with thick brick walls. Jesus was outside the tower, whispering His love for me, but the brick walls were screaming shame, guilt, and mistakes. I couldn't hear Jesus outside. I had built these walls believing I was keeping myself safe. Satan was on top of the tower, ready to push me back down inside the moment I tried to climb out.

Week five was testimony week. I sat in a room with fifty other young men and women, and we were supposed to tell our stories. You better believe I walked into that room that morning still believing Satan's lies that I was the worst person in the room, saying, "No way in this world am I talking today." I couldn't be more thankful for my brave classmates who, one by one, told their stories. I realized in that room, that very day, that I wasn't alone in mistakes and failures. That the walls I had built weren't protecting me; they were keeping me locked in my shame. These people sharing their stories helped me climb out of this cage I had built for myself. This day, I realized I truly could be forgiven. This was the day of breakthrough, the day that truth set me free.

I get overwhelmed when I look at the story of my life, how a perfect God could love and want me, a sinner, who so easily forgets what an awesome, all-powerful God He is!

> The Lord is my shepherd; I shall not want. He makes me to lie down in green pastures; He restores my soul; He leads me in paths of righteousness for His name's sake. (Psalm 23:1–3)

PRAYER

Lord, thank You. Thank You for being the God who restores all things and blesses Your children. Thank You for calling me Yours and for relentlessly pursuing me when all hope seemed lost.

....

continue your personal prayer

THE THIEF OF JOY

Ever feel like overwhelming blessings can be drowned out by overwhelming stress? Planning my wedding (especially from three thousand miles away) is probably one of the most stressful things I have ever done. But why? Why would I let this blessed day that I get to walk down the aisle to my forever become a curse? Isn't that the way Satan works? He takes something so wonderful and makes it a huge stress. I guarantee on that day I'm not going to care one bit what the decorations look like, or if everyone likes the music selection, or what anyone thinks. I'm going to be focused on the man I love; that is all that's going to matter to me! I need to stop being silly, take four deep breaths, and remember how much God is blessing me with this day. Maybe you're struggling with something stressful in life right now, or maybe you're simply having a hard time remembering the important things. The most important thing is making sure we love like Jesus.

> Love is patient, love is kind. It does not envy, it does not boast, it is not proud. It does not dishonor others, it is not self-seeking, it is not easily angered, it keeps no record of wrongs. Love does not delight in evil but rejoices with the truth. It always protects, always trusts, always hopes, always perseveres.
>
> Love never fails. But where there are prophecies, they will cease; where there are tongues, they will be stilled; where there is knowledge, it will pass away. For we know in part, and we prophesy in part, but when completeness comes, what is in part disappears.

When I was a child, I talked like a child, I thought like a child, I reasoned like a child. When I became a man, I put the ways of childhood behind me. For now we see only a reflection as in a mirror; then we shall see face to face. Now I know in part; then I shall know fully, even as I am fully known.

And now these three remain: faith, hope and love. But the greatest of these is love. (1 Corinthians 13:4–13)

PRAYER

Lord, build in me Your kind of love. Let me be focused on loving well.

....

....

....

....

....

....

....

....

....

continue your personal prayer

GLORIOUS DAY

(I wrote this one week after getting married to my sweet husband. It's funny to read things I wrote so long ago, but it's also so sweet to remember this time. I didn't completely rewrite this chapter, although I did take out some of the fluff, because of the wisdom and insight the Lord has blessed me with throughout the years of marriage and raising kiddos. But I wanted to leave the sweet, excited energy of the chapter. After you read the cheese, I'll have some meat at the end.)

I'm married! It's a lot to get used to.
I have to brag a little on my God! He knows what we need, guys! We have no reason to doubt His plan for our lives. His timing couldn't possibly be any better. We can trust Him! This past week (yes, I know; it's only been a week), I have been counting my blessings. God has blessed me so much with a man who couldn't be more perfect for me. My best friend, the person who makes me laugh uncontrollably even when I don't feel good. This man is the one God has had for me my whole life. God has brought us both through hard times and struggles, preparing us for our life together, showing us the blessing of each other is not to be taken for granted and proving Himself faithful!

Something really cool that I realized just before our wedding was that Chad and I had known each other and been together three months, three weeks, and three days on our wedding day. I did a study on the significance of the number three in the Bible, and this spoke to me of the finished work of redemption in Jesus Christ on the cross! He has made us new! We also will be celebrating Thanksgiving on our anniversary every seven years, another reminder of the completeness only God can supply in our relationship and our lives!

Our wedding was the most incredible day of my life but just the beginning of the revelation of God's redemptive work not only in my heart but also in my relationship with my dad and brother and my entire family! Through the ups and downs, God is always faithful. We are never too far gone to start over and be made new! Oh, how He blessed our day!

(Baylee from the future here to say I debated deleting this entire chapter, as it's silly to think about that starstruck girl who wrote it. Everything I wrote is still true today, more so in some ways! I've seen my husband become a father and three different times got to witness the miracle that is bringing forth another life from my body. I couldn't love my little family more. The funny part is to think about just one week into marriage writing about marriage. I knew nothing and still have a lot to learn. What I do know to be true is Jesus is the sustainer of life, and He's our only hope and joy. Often, I've looked to people, be it my husband, kids, or elsewhere, for that fulfillment, and it's only draining on them, much less impossible long-term. Jesus fills us and sustains us so we can be life to those around us. This is the only thing I'd remind this sweet girl.)

> For by Him all things were created that are in heaven and that are on earth, visible and invisible, whether thrones or dominions or principalities or powers. All things were created through Him and for Him. And He is before all things, and in Him all things consist. (Colossians 1:16–17)

PRAYER

Lord, thank You for Your continuous growth in my life. Fill me to overflowing with Your living water, that I might be a source of life.

LOVE DEEPER

In our society, we have such a skewed perception of marriage and love in general. From TV shows to celebrity news, everyone paints this picture of falling out of love as if it's just doomed to grow cold. Although I know this is the case unfortunately much of the time, I don't believe this has to be true. In the beginning of a relationship, love is a feeling. It's easy, warm, and fuzzy; it's fireworks and butterflies. Pretty soon, it's not that anymore; it becomes familiar and, if you let it, mundane. But that's the key. Love is a choice. You choose how things go, you choose to let other things get in the way of your relationship, or you choose not to. You choose to let things get stale and dull by neglecting your love, or you choose to prioritize and rekindle. I'm of the opinion that people don't simply fall out of love; they get lazy and stop pursuing the person they vowed to love for all their lives. People grow apart because they're not tying themselves together. Love is not selfish; love chooses others over itself. If love requires that you emphasize yourself over someone else, then it's simply not truly love. That is why the world's mantra to "love yourself so you can love others" is so silly to me. This is going to be a very unpopular sentiment, but I say this as a gentle truth. You already love yourself plenty. If you didn't, Jesus wouldn't have commanded you to "deny yourself." I'm convinced our marriage problems and just about every other relational issue we have in life would be rectified if we could get true, unselfish love figured out. The problem is, of course, that I am selfish by nature. I daily have to ask the Lord to reconstruct my thought process to not choose myself and my desires first. To put others before myself. This is a choice. It requires work, but it's also a certain way to have thriving relationships. Choosing ourselves all the time is a sure way to be miserable and a drain on others. Choosing to love and serve others exemplifies Jesus in every way.

> Let each of you look out not only for his own interests,
> but also for the interests of others. (Philippians 2:4)

PRAYER

Lord, let me love like You. Give me grace and let me live selflessly in service to others, just as You do for me.

....

....

....

....

....

....

....

....

....

....

continue your personal prayer

YOUR OWN SALVATION

Sometimes I catch myself looking at others and thinking about how they say or do certain things with no conviction, when I myself have been strongly convinced those things are sin. I tend to judge in my heart those people who struggle or are blind or simply aren't at that place in their walk with Jesus yet. Don't get me wrong. There are things that are black and white in the Bible as sin, but there are gray areas that can manifest as personal convictions. As believers, Jesus is taking us all on the journey toward holiness. This is a journey that only ends in heaven. We all have different starting points, and therefore, the journey looks different for us all.

The Bible tells us in Philippians 2:12–13 to "work out your own salvation with fear and trembling; for it is God who works in you both to will and to do for His good pleasure."

In 1 Thessalonians 4:11a, it says to "make it your ambition to lead a quiet life: You should mind your own business …"

In Romans 12:3, "Do not think of yourself more highly than you ought, but rather think of yourself with sober judgment, in accordance with the faith God has distributed to each of you."

In other words, but also in the same words, mind your own business, for it's God who works any good in your life anyway! I am nothing but a sinner, and when I start to compare myself to others, I can be certain I'm in sin, because there is nothing good in me. Comparison is the fruit of pride, and pride is all about self, and by myself, I'm in big trouble!

PRAYER

Lord, give me a sober view of who I am on my own. Help me to view others in the same light, for You paid the same price for us all. Let us love one another.

··

··

··

··

··

··

··

··

··

··

··

··

continue your personal prayer

I WANT TO BLESS

Finally, brethren, whatever things are true, whatever things *are* noble, whatever things *are* just, whatever things *are* pure, whatever things *are* lovely, whatever things *are* of good report, if *there is* any virtue and if *there is* anything praiseworthy—meditate on these things. The things which you learned and received and heard and saw in me, these do, and the God of peace will be with you.
—Philippians 4:8–9

I know I have written about these verses often, because it's such a huge reminder to me of how important it is to meditate on the things of God. As Christians, sometimes I feel there is a temptation to see how close I can walk to the world, enjoying the things of the world, and still be a Christian. How much more blessed we are as well as a blessing to others when we focus on the things of God, remembering that with which we fill ourselves is what we will pour out. I want to pour out the things that are lovely and pure rather than the things that are selfish, perverse, and evil. In order to be righteous and bless those around me, I must fill myself with righteousness.

PRAYER

Lord, be my filling. When I'm pressed, when I feel stretched, be what pours out of me. Give me wisdom for filling myself wholesomely at Your well, and let me stand up to the temptation to fill myself elsewhere.

THE TRUE LOVE LETTER

I feel like it is so easy to fall into a religious way of doing things. I once heard a good comparison. If the love of your life wrote you a letter declaring their love to you, would you have to carve out or schedule time to read that letter? Would you sit down and have to block out everything else, focusing on every word just to get something out of it and make sure your mind didn't wander to other things? No. You would hang on every word in that letter because the person you love wrote it to declare their love to you! You would happily, excitedly give that letter all of your attention, reading it two, three, maybe four times. You would get that warm feeling, those butterflies inside. That is how God desires us to read the Bible. It's not a *have to*; it should be a *want to*, an exciting thing to read the greatest love letter ever written, and it's written to us. It's a love story of sacrifice, forgiveness, grace, and perfect love, written by the true love of our lives, the literal *creator* of love. Yet all too often, it becomes just part of my routine, something I need to do. My prayer is that I can grasp just how much His Word and love means and hold onto to the excitement that the God of the universe loves and wants me.

> But You, O Lord, *are* a God full of compassion, and gracious, Long suffering and abundant in mercy and truth. (Psalm 86:15)

PRAYER

Lord, my heart is deceitfully wicked. I'm incapable of choosing You on my own. Let my heart fall deeply in love with You! Let my heart seek to be closer to You. Set my heart on fire, burning for You and You alone.

continue your personal prayer

THE BIG QUESTION—WHY?

You know that feeling of déjà vu, like *I think I've been here before?* It's been happening to me spiritually a lot lately. The question this morning once again was "Why do you do what you do?" I was gracefully broken when I humbly came to the honest answer in my soul, which was "You have the wrong motivation." Whether it's writing these devotionals or reading my Bible, I find myself doing it either to be seen by others or out of religious duty. Just yesterday, the message to my heart was "Find the true love in His love letter to us." This morning's motivation was similar, followed by the realization that I am focused once again on how I am perceived, instead of doing this for the glory of God and because I feel He has asked me to. Even if not one single person reads this book in my lifetime, I should be focused on the fact that my Savior has asked me to do this, so I'm going to do it.

I heard a great analogy this morning that really hit home.

There was once a king who loved his wife. When she died, he wanted to build a tomb for her. He put her casket in the center and began to build this incredible structure around her. It took years to build it. When it was finally finished, it came time to dedicate the tomb to his wife, but they couldn't find the casket anywhere. During the time of the build, the casket got in the way, so they needed to move it outside, and when it got in the way outside, it got moved farther from the build, until it finally got moved so far away that it got taken to the dump.

If I'm not careful, I can start to do something for the glory of the Lord. This mission starts out beautifully and with pure intent and motive, focused fully on glorifying God. Then I simply lose sight of the true reason I started to do it in the first place.

> And whatever you do in word or deed, do all in the name of the Lord Jesus, giving thanks to God the Father through Him. (Colossians 3:17)

PRAYER

Lord, let the motivation of my heart be to live to honor You completely. It's all about You, Lord.

....

....

....

....

....

....

....

....

....

continue your personal prayer

WRETCHED TO PRICELESS

Sometimes I get overwhelmed when I look at the grace, mercy, and sovereignty of my God. Recently, I was blessed to have the opportunity to give my testimony to a group of teen girls. It amazes me that God could take a messed-up sinner like me and wash me white as snow, leaving my old life, my old self, so far away that when I give my testimony, it feels like a dead person in history that I'm telling a story about! His forgiveness has allowed me to live without shame or regret, to live free! Of course, I have to surrender my old self and shame to God again from time to time, but it's amazing and humbling not only that He can but that He will and that He did take and restore my life! We are never too far from His forgiveness and restoration. All we have to do is call on His name, admitting that we are wretched sinners, that we can't do it without Him. For me, it was a long, prideful, stubborn journey of pain and trying to do this life on my own. I still haven't got anything figured out and can definitely plan on bumps along the way, but this one thing I do know for sure: I need Jesus! Today, tomorrow, every second of every minute of every day! Only He can make this dull stone a priceless jewel!

> "Now, therefore," says the Lord,
> "Turn to Me with all your heart,
> With fasting, with weeping, and with mourning."
> So rend your heart, and not your garments;
> Return to the Lord your God,

For He *is* gracious and merciful,
Slow to anger, and of great kindness;
And He relents from doing harm. (Joel 2:12–13)

PRAYER

Lord, You're the one who makes me. Please keep doing Your work until I enter Your kingdom.

....

....

....

....

....

....

....

....

....

....

....

continue your personal prayer

BE STRONG AND VERY COURAGEOUS

In the first chapter of Joshua, we see that he is told four times to "be strong and very courageous." I believe this is because he was one man about to create an army and face every city in his region. He must have been afraid. But as we read, we see that he did indeed take this command to heart. He did trust in the Lord, and as he did so, we see he conquered city after city, king after king. The Lord strengthened his faith and fought for him, but he first had to step out in faith. He first had to put his faith in God and trust that he was more powerful than all the kings and armies Joshua would face. In chapter 10, we see the phrase "and the Lord fought for Israel" or "and the Lord delivered" four times. We also see Joshua giving the same command to his army to "be strong and courageous." Joshua couldn't have commanded this with confidence if he was still afraid. He had been through the fight and had seen the Lord deliver his enemy into his hand. His faith had been strengthened through using it. Joshua can now say with confidence to not be afraid because he knows God will see him through.

Maybe you're in a fearful place right now. Be strong and very courageous. Take courage in the one who will go before you, who will fight on your behalf. Use your faith and watch it grow when your enemy or your problem is defeated before your eyes. It may be in the eternal life to come, but He will make all things right. Take courage in this truth!

"These things I have spoken to you, that in Me you may have peace. In the world you will have tribulation; but be of good cheer, I have overcome the world." (John 16:33)

PRAYER

Lord, I'm certain with You the battle is already won. When You fight on my behalf, I don't have to wonder who's in control. Strengthen my faith, Lord, I pray!

....

....

....

....

....

....

....

....

....

....

continue your personal prayer

DRAW ME CLOSE
TO YOU

"God, I want to be close to You. I want to be where it's safe. I feel so far from Your hand, and it's scary."

For many weeks now, I've been struggling off and on with feeling distant from the Lord. So many new attacks come and go, but I never really take the time to pray for Him to draw me near. Chad shared he had been feeling the same way. Praying in repentance this morning, we opened up the Bible to 2 Thessalonians, chapter 1.

Grace to you and peace from God our Father and the Lord Jesus Christ.

> We are bound to thank God always for you, brethren, as it is fitting, because your faith grows exceedingly, and the love of every one of you all abounds toward each other, so that we ourselves boast of you among the churches of God for your patience and faith in all your persecutions and tribulations that you endure, *which is* manifest evidence of the righteous judgment of God, that you may be counted worthy of the kingdom of God, for which you also suffer. (2 Thessalonians 1:2–5)

God uses tribulations to draw us closer to Him, to grow in us love and empathy for one another. Suffering is never a fun thing, but it is so important that we remember to count the suffering joyous, for it is growth of righteousness, and it is the evidence that we are counted worthy of the kingdom of God. How much more joy should that bring to us to know that these attacks are strengthening our spiritual muscles.

> Therefore we also pray always for you that our God would count you worthy of *this* calling, and fulfill all the good pleasure of *His* goodness and the work of faith with power, that the name of our Lord Jesus Christ may be glorified in you, and you in Him, according to the grace of our God and the Lord Jesus Christ. (2 Thessalonians 1:11–12)

PRAYER

Lord, all I want my life to say about me is that the work of God was fulfilled in it. All I want is to be counted worthy in Your sight, and because of Jesus, I am. I want You to be glorified in what I say and do. This is my prayer, and though I fail constantly, though distractions creep in and steal my focus, I pray that I go through and grow through all the struggles. I want to praise You in every season and know Your hand and Your perfect plan is in everything.

....

....

....

....

....

....

continue your personal prayer

GIVE THANKS
FOR IT ALL

Therefore, I exhort first of all that supplications, prayers,
intercessions and giving of thanks be made for all men,
for kings and all who are in authority, that we may lead a
quiet and peaceable life in all godliness and reverence.
—1 Timothy 1:1–2

"Give thanks for all men." Give thanks for all men? It's easy to give thanks for our friends and family, the people who bring joy into our hearts and lives. But isn't it hard sometimes to thank God for the people who make life a little harder, the ones who drive us a little looney? It's mesmerizing to take ahold of the Holy Spirit's power in those moments. In Him, we have the ability to give thanks for the person standing right in front of us, no matter how difficult, to realize that these people in our lives are the tools God is using to knock off the rough edges. We need to be chiseled in some areas so we all fit together with our brothers and sisters perfectly in heaven. God uses each of us in each other's lives to build in us His character and possibly to change someone's life. We may be the only glimpse of Jesus a person ever sees in their lives. As soon as we see the people around us as a blessing from God, either to grow us or to pour out His love to, our entire attitude toward all people will change, and we will automatically fulfill His other commandments of being quiet, peaceful, godly, and reverent—content. For it's hard to be thankful and discontent at the same time.

PRAYER

Lord, please change my heart. Give me compassion and love for all, as I know You love and died for every living person. Let me see them as You see them, as You see me.

....

....

....

....

....

....

....

....

....

....

....

....

....

continue your personal prayer

REFLECTIONS

I started 2017 out just ending, without a doubt, the worst year of my life. I was heartbroken, and, simply put, I was the empty shell of the person I used to be, with no hope of my life ever being good again. My parents didn't really want me around, and I can't say that I blamed them. The relationship I had just ended was very toxic but secret. Because no one knew about this relationship, my family had only seen the tailspin I was in, without knowing the cause. They didn't know the hurt going on in my private life. They only saw the side effects of the hurt I was feeling deep inside. I was a liar. I was selfish and miserable. Like a wounded animal, I was mean. I had all but ruined my relationship with my older brother, who, for most of my life, was my best friend. Worse yet, I was convinced my God was absolutely done with me as well. I was too far from forgiveness, for sure. I had to go, had to get away from the sorrowful life I had created. I left my home in Texas and headed for YWAM (Youth with a Mission) in Mazatlán, Mexico. I experienced God's grace, love, and forgiveness in such a profound way—a way I could never have experienced had I not felt so alone and in such dire need of Him. To see the way God has used my story to speak with authority on His character has been powerful to me.

Fast-forward seven years. This year, I'll celebrate my seven-year wedding anniversary with the love of my life. We've had three beautiful children, and I can say without a doubt He can renew and restore anyone. Although the path I took was not God's best, it has been amazing to see how He uses the broken, the weak, and the foolish of this earth, even me, the lowliest, a very simple sinner, for His glory. He can wash us white as snow. We just have to let Him.

I'm still alive, so I still anticipate many mistakes along the way, but Jesus will continue His work in me, and if you're in Him, He's not done with you either! No matter where you're at today, He's right there with you.

> Being confident of this very thing, that He who has begun a good work in you will complete *it* until the day of Jesus Christ. (Philippians 1:6)

PRAYER

Lord, I know You paid it all. Help my heart to feel it, for my soul to realize fully that I do not have to live in shame. Give my heart a place to rest.

....

....

....

....

....

....

....

....

....

continue your personal prayer

THE HEART

During an entire nine days of being sick with the flu, I had a lot of time to think. I thought a lot about Mexico, how life there was spent being aware of others, having a heart to serve God and others all the time. I find it hard to believe how quickly I can lose sight of what matters most in life, and that truly is serving God and others. But how do I do that here in normal life? I mean, sure it's easy when your attending class six hours of the day, where your primary focus is God and others, but what about here? What about when your primary focus is folding clothes, washing dishes, and cooking dinner? How do I do anything that matters? The answer is in my heart. Our hearts are the only things Jesus judges; therefore, it is the only thing with which we need to be right before Him. Our actions can be good, generous, seemingly loving, and kind, but if our heart is wrong or selfish, then our actions don't matter to God in the least. We can be certain, like the Pharisees, that the applause of men is all we'll receive.

Reading Hebrews 4, I was reminded that my God sees everything.

> For the word of God *is* living and powerful, and sharper than any two-edged sword, piercing even to the division of soul and spirit, and of joints and marrow, and is a discerner of the thoughts and intents of the heart. And there is no creature hidden from His sight, but all things *are* naked and open to the eyes of Him to whom we *must give* account. (Hebrews 4:12–13)

We are called to do everything without murmuring or complaining (Philippians 2:14) to the God who sees everything. Even if I'm not complaining with my words, my heart could still be ugly.

Serving, no matter who it is, with a clean, joyful, happy heart shows a sensitivity to the character of God and shows a reverence for the gift He has given me.

Serving joyfully in all situations, in every moment, whether seen by others or seen only by God, that is how I can live an extraordinary life.

PRAYER

Lord, give me a happy heart to serve. Let everything I do, whether mundane or extraordinary, be done unto You with a pure heart and conscience.

....

....

....

....

....

....

....

....

continue your personal prayer

PRAYING WITH SINCERITY

"And when you pray, you shall not be like the hypocrites.
For they love to pray standing in the synagogues and on
the corners of the streets, that they may be seen by men.
Assuredly, I say to you, they have their reward. But you, when
you pray, go into your room, and when you have shut your
door, pray to your Father who *is* in the secret *place;* and your
Father who sees in secret will reward you openly. And when
you pray, do not use vain repetitions as the heathen *do.* For
they think that they will be heard for their many words.
"Therefore do not be like them. For your Father
knows the things you have need of before you
ask Him. In this manner, therefore, pray:
"Our Father in heaven, Hallowed be Your name. Your
kingdom come, Your will be done on earth as *it is* in
heaven. Give us this day our daily bread. And forgive us our
debts, as we forgive our debtors. And do not lead us into
temptation but deliver us from the evil one. For Yours is the
kingdom and the power and the glory forever. Amen.
"For if you forgive men their trespasses, your heavenly Father
will also forgive you. But if you do not forgive men their
trespasses, neither will your Father forgive your trespasses."
—Matthew 6:5–15

I am reminded to treat my relationship with my Lord as I would
any other relationship. I wouldn't speak to my husband with great,

elaborate words. I wouldn't say his name a hundred times in one sentence. He wouldn't feel very loved if I was looking out of the corner of my eye, saying things in beautiful poetry so that everyone listening would hear me and think that I was a good wife. No, I wouldn't care what anyone else thought. I love my husband. I speak to him with clear sincerity because I have a sincere relationship with him. This is how God desires me to speak to Him as well, to speak sincerely, not using elaborate religious words to sound good to men, not saying His name at the end and beginning of every sentence but praying to God as we would speak to our dad, our friend, or our love. God desires sincere love. He already knows our heart before we speak. If our hearts are not sincere, it doesn't matter what our mouths say.

PRAYER

Lord, I pray for a sincere heart and pure motivation with everything I do in my life. Fill me with Your Spirit, I pray!

....

....

....

....

....

....

continue your personal prayer

THE PLANK
IN MY EYE

And why do you look at the speck in your brother's eye, but do not consider the plank in your own eye? Or how can you say to your brother, 'Let me remove the speck from your eye'; and look, a plank *is* in your own eye? Hypocrite! First remove the plank from your own eye, and then you will see clearly to remove the speck from your brother's eye.
—Matthew 7:3–5

It's so much easier for me to see and judge the things other people struggle with. It's so much easier to judge them for their actions and myself by my intentions. What a hypocrite I am! I hate the things I struggle with so much that a lot of times I can be living in denial of them. The closer you are to an object, the harder it is to see it clearly. Similarly, at times, the more prevalent a sin is in my life, the more it has just become a habit, the harder it is to see it clearly. Take gossiping as an example. If I become comfortable with talking about other people in my life, it can easily become a habit. I might not even fully notice when I'm doing it. But this might be glaringly obvious to me when others do it. Lying, cursing, or coveting could be used in the same example. The things I judge so quickly in other people are usually the things I struggle with the most. I tend to have a lot more grace (or excuses) for myself in sin than I do when judging someone else. I've heard it said, "My sin looks so much worse on you."

When we are living in hypocrisy instead of allowing the Lord to do His work in our hearts, we end up beating our brother or sister with the plank in our eyes. Imagine having a log sticking out of your eye and trying to get close enough to remove the speck from someone else's! We must first overcome our own sins in order to assist others, and the only way to overcome sin is with the power of Jesus and His Holy Spirit within us.

PRAYER

Jesus, I pray that You will reveal and take away these things from my life, and the judgmental attitude with them! I want my life to fully reflect You, and I know the only way I can accomplish this is to fill myself to the brim with Your love, to meditate on the character I would like my life to exude, in You alone.

....

....

....

....

....

....

....

....

....

continue your personal prayer

WHICH ARE YOU FEEDING MORE?

The spiritual war going on inside our hearts can be likened to a dog fight, a black dog representing our flesh and a white dog representing our spirit. The winner is determined by which one we feed the most.

I know this is an ever-recurring message throughout this book. But this is a message I believe is too important not to be reminded of constantly. Christians, even prominent leaders in the body of Christ today, are being taken down, annihilated by the enemy, and many nonbelievers are pushed further from the saving knowledge of Jesus as a result. We are in a spiritual battle where the enemy never takes a break. Sure, there may be seasons of smooth sailing and little spiritual fights going on, but the enemy is always strategizing, always watching for areas of weakness or places fit for attack. The lulls in the fight aren't so much the enemy taking a holiday as they are time to get an ambush laid out. We are not to be in fear of the enemy. Jesus has already won this fight, but we are to be wise. We are to be putting on the full armor of God (Ephesians 6:10–18). We are to be within our protection, arming our souls with truth, training our hearts in the ways of Jesus so that when temptation from the enemy does strike, we are ready to withstand. I don't believe it can be overstated; you are in a battle with an enemy that hates your soul. Satan wants *nothing* more than to see you burn in hell for eternity. He is evil. He hates us. Playing with his vices isn't a game. It isn't cute. We invite him closer to us every time we engage with something designed to sear our conscience. Sin isn't bad because it's forbidden;

it's forbidden because it's bad. Jesus knows the damage sin does, and because He loves us, He tells us to stay away from it. Starve the flesh. Feed the spirit. When we do this, we won't have to wonder which will win the war.

> Be sober, be vigilant; because your adversary the devil walks about like a roaring lion, seeking whom he may devour. (1 Peter 5:8)

PRAYER

Lord, give me wisdom. Let me crave the things of You and be repulsed by the things of this world. Train me with Your truth.

....

....

....

....

....

....

....

....

....

continue your personal prayer

FAITH CHANGES THINGS

Then behold, they brought to Him a paralytic lying on a
bed. When Jesus saw their faith, He said to the paralytic,
"Son, be of good cheer; your sins are forgiven you."
And at once some of the scribes said within
themselves, "This Man blasphemes!"
But Jesus, knowing their thoughts, said, "Why do you think
evil in your hearts? For which is easier, to say, '*Your* sins are
forgiven you,' or to say, 'Arise and walk'? But that you may
know that the Son of Man has power on earth to forgive sins"—
then He said to the paralytic, "Arise, take up your bed, and
go to your house." And he arose and departed to his house.
Now when the multitudes saw *it,* they marveled and
glorified God, who had given such power to men.
—Matthew 9:2–8

This account is not specific on who the *they* are, but when we
look at this account in Luke 5 (18–25), we see that "they" refers
to the paralyzed man's friends and that they didn't just simply bring
him before Jesus; they desperately brought him. They tore off the
roof of the house Jesus was in because it was too crowded. They got
ropes and lowered their friend through the roof before Jesus. They
did this because they loved their friend and believed Jesus could heal
him. And it says when Jesus saw their faith, *their* faith, He healed
the paralyzed man. But He didn't just heal him. First, He forgave
his sins.

My grandmother used to be the manager of a fairgrounds. Every year during the carnival or when a concert was held at the fairgrounds, my grandma would hook us up with endless free ride passes or a VIP backstage meeting with the singer. All of us grandkids felt like big shots. We had the connections. We felt special when we could walk into her office and behind the counter anytime because that was our grandma.

How much more of a connection do we have when we hook up our friends with the lifeline that is Jesus. We have the opportunity to bring our friends before Him every day, every moment in prayer. How often do we? Do we love our friends so dearly that we're willing to blow the roof off in prayer for them? Do we believe that Jesus has the power to heal them, the power to change and transform their lives? It doesn't say that Jesus saw the faith of the paralyzed man, and because of it, He healed him; it was the faith of his friends. The man had no way of getting to Jesus unless his friends brought him. We need to bring the friends who have no other way of getting there. We need to lift them up and lower them in front of the one who can heal. Our faith can change things for those around us.

PRAYER

Lord, let me see them. Let me see those in need. Let me be a prayer warrior for those in need. Let me be looking out for my friends. Let me be lifting them up.

....

....

....

....

continue your personal prayer

WHEN SIN IS
REVEALED

This morning, God revealed my heart to me. Oh how ugly and gross it can be when it gets clogged with sin, and the illness of sin is everywhere. I so easily get infected with it. I sincerely long to be used by God. He starts to answer my prayers by using my life, and then my heart desires the selfish glory. Sometimes I can see the pride start to well up in me. I can see the ugliness that it causes in my speech and my life. I recognize it as the putrid sin it is, but how hopeless I am if I try to fix it on my own. Sometimes I actually say to myself very sternly, "Why did you say that negative thing? Don't be negative anymore!" Or "That wasn't glorifying to God. Don't do that, or think that, or say that anymore!" But what do I find myself doing ten minutes later? That exact same thing. Paul talks about this in Romans in a tongue twister type way:

> I do not understand what I do. For what I want to do I do not do, but what I hate I do. And if I do what I do not want to do, I agree that the law is good. As it is, it is no longer I myself who do it, but it is sin living in me. For I know that good itself does not dwell in me, that is, in my sinful nature. For I have the desire to do what is good, but I cannot carry it out. For I do not do the good I want to do, but the evil I do not want to do—this I keep on doing. Now if I do what I do not want to do, it is no longer I who do it, but it is sin living in me that does it. (Romans 7:15–20)

It's amazing how even doing what God has called you to do can start out being done for His glory and then quickly become something for your own selfish gain, done with the wrong motivation. It is a continuous process, a continuous cycle of growth and change. It's a slower change than I like, but we can be sure He is constantly working on our hearts.

PRAYER

Lord, I pray for a pure heart and a renewed mind. I pray for Your kingdom to be furthered through me and not my desire for my own kingdom. I pray for You to cleanse the sin of selfishness from my life and for me to pick up my cross daily in humble service to You, Lord. For we know from that scripture that the only good in me is from You. I must give my life to You daily in order for any good to flow from it.

....

....

....

....

....

....

....

continue your personal prayer

YOU FEED THEM

When Jesus heard *it,* He departed from there by boat to a deserted place by Himself. But when the multitudes heard it, they followed Him on foot from the cities. And when Jesus went out He saw a great multitude; and He was moved with compassion for them, and healed their sick. When it was evening, His disciples came to Him, saying, "This is a deserted place, and the hour is already late. Send the multitudes away, that they may go into the villages and buy themselves food." But Jesus said to them, "They do not need to go away. You give them something to eat." And they said to Him, "We have here only five loaves and two fish." He said, "Bring them here to Me." Then He commanded the multitudes to sit down on the grass. And He took the five loaves and the two fish, and looking up to heaven, He blessed and broke and gave the loaves to the disciples; and the disciples gave to the multitudes. So they all ate and were filled, and they took up twelve baskets full of the fragments that remained. Now those who had eaten were about five thousand men, besides women and children.
—Matthew 14:13–21

"They don't need to go away. You give them something to eat." This sentence jumped out at me. Jesus gives the disciples the opportunity to perform this miracle by commanding them to "give them something to eat." They had seen Jesus perform so many miracles before. Had the disciples just said, "Okay, Lord. I don't know how, but we will feed them," Jesus would have used them to execute this miracle. But instead, they say, "We can't. It's impossible." If I would just believe that God is the God He says He is, the God of miracles, I would be able to be a part of performing more of His miracles, but instead, I'm usually the one who says, "It's impossible. I can't do it." Luckily for us, Jesus doesn't change just because we struggle to trust. When we doubt, He says, "Well, no, *you* can't, but *I* surely can. Bring them to me."

There are so many accounts in the Old Testament of people saying, "Okay, God, I don't know how You'll do this, but I'll do what You tell me. I'll step out in faith." And they watch as the walls of a great and mighty city falls (Joshua 6), or the giant is defeated (1 Samuel 17), or all your people are saved through you (Esther 8), just to name a few …

I want to be the person who says, "Okay. I don't know how, but I'll allow You to direct me. If You're in it, I know I'll see a miracle." I want to *be* the person to step out in faith and see the power of God manifested in my life rather than just reading about those giants in the faith.

PRAYER

Lord, You never change. You're still the God of miracles we see throughout the Bible. Use my life how You see fit. Give me courage to step out and obey even when I don't understand.

....

....

....

....

continue your personal prayer

DO YOU WANT TO BE GREAT? YOU SURE?

You know when God is teaching you something that goes completely against your human nature, something so close to your heart that you don't really want to talk about it? Something you don't really even want to openly acknowledge? That is what's been happening in me these past few weeks. A servant's heart is something I've prayed for before, but once I realized how He was answering that prayer and how hard it is to learn to be meek and humble, because it comes through humiliation and being treated like a slave, I was quick to say, "Hey, never mind. I was just kidding!"

I've heard it said, "The best way to judge whether you have a servant's heart or not is how you act when people treat you like one."

Reading through Matthew these past few weeks, I have been reminded time and again that the meek, the humble, the servant, the least here on earth will be the greatest in heaven.

I read it on paper, and my heart says, "Yes! I want to be the least! I want to be humble!" But then how do I act when someone walks across the street in front of my car as if she's on a Sunday stroll, figuratively stopping to smell the flowers, without so much as eye contact to say, "Thanks"? Or when someone speeds past me on the road, shaking their head in disbelief that I'm going the speed limit. Then, because they're so focused on showing me how they feel, they don't realize the car in front of them has stopped and at the last minute cut me off, forcing me to slam on my breaks as my water cup goes flying on to the floor of my truck? Just a few examples from recent experiences. The meek, humble, patient, servant character does not shine through in these moments. But these are the moments teaching me to be more patient, to pray for a heart more like Christ.

When we pray for patience, a servant's heart, or humility, we should be prepared to exercise our patience, serve as a slave, or be humiliated! How else can we build those muscles in that character if we don't use it? I can honestly say I want to be greatest in heaven! That means I must be lowest here on earth, which means I better be prepared to be tested in these areas.

> "But whoever desires to become great among you, let him be your servant. And whoever desires to be first among you, let him be your slave— just as the Son of Man did not come to be served, but to serve, and to give His life a ransom for many." (Matthew 20:26b–28)

PRAYER

Lord, though I know these prayers will bring trials, give me strength to pray them anyway. Let me grow more like You!

....

....

....

....

....

....

continue your personal prayer

MY ICKY TONGUE

If anyone among you thinks he is religious, and does not bridle his tongue but deceives his own heart, this one's religion *is* useless.
—James 1:26

Oh, tongue, you are a pesky, little contrivance. Sometimes I wish someone would just cut mine out. I could just nod my head for yes and shake it for no. But since it's not going anywhere, I better learn how to use it.

Proverbs 18:21 says, "Death and life *are in* the power of the tongue, And those who love it will eat its fruit."

How picky am I about the fruit I eat? I want sweet, crisp, delicious, delightful fruit. If it's not good, I'm quick to throw it in the trash. What's better than a piece of fruit on a hot day? It's healthy. No regret after eating it because you know you're doing something good for your body. If I treated the words I speak as if they were fruit I'd have to eat later, how much more calculated would I be with the words I chose? I would examine them like an apple I was about to eat, making sure there wasn't any rottenness or holes from bugs.

After all, who wants to eat bitter, rotten, wormy fruit? No one. But how often do my words figuratively set my fruit out in the sun to rot? Throw it to the worms? Too often. Oh how I desire to glorify God with this dangerous little instrument in my mouth.

PRAYER

Lord, I pray that You will speak through me, that my life will produce tasty fruit to feed the body of Christ.

LET ME BE A MASTER OF REPENTANCE

> Now as they were eating, He said, "Assuredly, I
> say to you, one of you will betray Me."
> And they were exceedingly sorrowful, and each of
> them began to say to Him, "Lord, is it I?"
> He answered and said, "He who dipped *his* hand with
> Me in the dish will betray Me. The Son of Man indeed
> goes just as it is written of Him, but woe to that man
> by whom the Son of Man is betrayed! It would have
> been good for that man if he had not been born."
> Then Judas, who was betraying Him,
> answered and said, "Rabbi, is it I?"
> He said to him, "You have said it."
> —Matthew 26:21–25

I am in awe of the grace of Jesus. He tells Judas, "I know what you're doing. I'm not blind to your plan." He shows Judas once again who He really is, the all-knowing Son of God, giving Judas every opportunity to repent, to change his mind. We may not have a plan to betray Jesus, but He does this with us too. He convicts us that what we are about to say is gossip, or what we are about to do does not glorify Him, but how many times, like Judas, do I continue with my plan? My prayer today and every day is that God will make me a master of repentance. That I will see Him for who He is, who I truly know Him to be. That if what I am about to do is against Him, I will fall at His feet and be broken when I see that my plan is not what He would have me do. We can repent at any moment.

PRAYER

Lord, let me be quick to repent, to change direction when I'm tempted to go down the wrong path. Let me run back to You.

....

....

....

....

....

....

....

....

....

....

....

....

continue your personal prayer

TO EACH ONE FOR THE PROFIT OF ALL

I think it is important for us to remember God has given spiritual gifts to each and every person who knows Him. Some have many gifts, and some have few, but He expects us to use what we have been given to further His kingdom. For He says,

> "Because it has been given to you to know the mysteries of the kingdom of heaven, but to them it has not been given. For whoever has, to him more will be given, and he will have abundance; but whoever does not have, even what he has will be taken away from him." (Matthew 13:11b–12)

He says, "It has been *given* to you." This knowledge has been *given* as a gift is *given*. If we don't use our gifts, they will be taken away. It is very important that we find out what we have been gifted with spiritually—and even more important that we use those gifts for His name's sake. For who is faithful with what he has, more will be given. It breaks my heart to hear children of God believing the lie of the enemy, that they have no gifts and therefore cannot be used by the Father. If you're in Christ, He has given You a specific gift for a specific purpose.

> There are diversities of gifts, but the same Spirit. There are differences of ministries, but the same Lord. And there are diversities of activities, but it is the same

God who works all in all. But the manifestation of the Spirit is given to each one for the profit *of all:* for to one is given the word of wisdom through the Spirit, to another the word of knowledge through the same Spirit, to another faith by the same Spirit, to another gifts of healings by the same Spirit, to another the working of miracles, to another prophecy, to another discerning of spirits, to another *different* kinds of tongues, to another the interpretation of tongues. But one and the same Spirit works all these things, distributing to each one individually as He wills. (1 Corinthians 12:4–11)

"To each one." Each child of God has been given a spiritual gift. If you don't know what your spiritual gifts are, ask a strong Christian mentor in your life. If you don't have a mentor in your life, you need to get one. People are just people, but just like iron sharpens iron, so one person sharpens another (Proverbs 27:17). Calling out the gifts and strengths in one another is so important for us to help each other grow! We need to get good at encouraging and admonishing our brothers and sisters in Christ.

PRAYER

Lord, reveal and strengthen the gifts You have given to me. Let me use those gifts for the purpose You have put me on this earth to accomplish.

....

....

....

continue your personal prayer

HELLO, LORD?

Teacher, do You not care that we are perishing?
—Mark 4:38b

Do you ever feel like God is asleep at the wheel? Like He doesn't even care that you feel overwhelmed by the storm?

> Then He arose and rebuked the wind, and said to the sea, "Peace, be still!" And the wind ceased and there was a great calm. But He said to them, "Why are you so fearful? How *is it* that you have no faith?" (Mark 4:39–40)

When I fully grasp who Jesus is and what He is capable of, I will not be afraid of the storm. I may not understand the storm, but I won't have to fear it.

Lately, my husband and I feel like we have been in a storm. It's a strange one, a storm of attacks on all levels of life and doubts that we know in our hearts are not true. It can feel like chaos is all around us, and it is. Winds of questions and waves of doubt beat against our little boat, and at times, it feels like Jesus is asleep. "Where in the world are You, Lord? Do you not care that we are drowning?" I can see Jesus smile at this question. "How can you still not believe? You know who I am. You have seen Me work. You know I have a plan; these storms are just so I can show My power in your life."

I'm learning at the pace of a sloth that He is always incredibly trustworthy. I don't have to understand how or why He does things the way He does, but I do have to remind myself daily, and sometimes hourly, that He is in control. He is a good, good Father, and He is not going to let me drown. He is *always* faithful.

PRAYER

Lord, let me trust in Your sovereignty over it all. I may not understand what's happening, but You are not worried. You may very well be metaphorically asleep in the boat, as You aren't worried about anything.

....

....

....

....

....

....

....

....

....

....

continue your personal prayer

STAGES OF LIFE

Sometimes I feel overwhelmed by my own mind. My morning devotionals used to be a glorious time of rest and refuge in the Lord, but lately it just feels like a raging storm of thoughts that I have to fight through to even hear Jesus speak.

In Mexico, I got a beautiful, incredible mountaintop experience of peace and rest for three whole months. A time to spend every waking moment fixed on the thoughts of my Lord and Savior. I got another three months of growing in insane amounts by putting into practice the work of the disciples, truly and tangibly getting to physically see God move and work. I left Mexico praying that I would never go back to a stagnant, dull life. That I would never backslide. That I would always live life abundantly.

I sit here praying, feeling as though I have backslid. This last month has been a fight to even hear God's voice through all the noise, busyness, and angst of life. He reminded me that, although like Moses, He allows us to come up the mountain and speak face-to-face with Him, there are times we need to go through the desert, to learn obedience in a different way, to gain character and understanding in areas we would have missed on the mountain. It's not that we've slid back into our old ways. If we're truly pressing into God, He is only moving us forward. Growth happens in all stages of life—on the mountains, through the prairies, and in the deserts. Sometimes it feels like touching the stars. Other times, it feels like pulling the weeds, and still others, it feels like digging for water in the thirsty land. I'm in the stage of digging right now, pressing in deep to hear the voice of my Lord, and He reminded me this day that I'm exactly where He wants me.

Blessed are those who hunger and thirst for righteousness, For they shall be filled. (Matthew 5:6)

Come to Me, all you who labor and are heavy laden, and I will give you rest. (Matthew 11:28)

PRAYER

Lord, let me press my roots down deep in You. Let me hear your voice clearly. Grow me. Let me rest in Your finished work for me. You're not done with me.

....

....

....

....

....

....

....

....

....

continue your personal prayer

UNGRATEFULNESS IS THE THIEF OF JOY

Behold what manner of love the Father has bestowed
on us, that we should be called children of God!
—1 John 3:1

This verse convicted my ungrateful heart. I realize how much grace God has shown me just by simply calling me His child, by dying in my place a brutal death for the chance that I might choose Him in return. When I actually try to grasp in my finite mind His love for me, I'm overwhelmed by His goodness. On top of all of that, I count all the blessings He's given me in life—a house, a vehicle, family, friends, a husband who loves me, my sweet, healthy children, an opportunity for ministry. I think of all the simple blessings I have been given by a God who calls me His daughter for no reason other than He wanted to. He doesn't owe me anything. I haven't been abundantly faithful to Him. I have betrayed Him. I have spat in His face and thrown His love back at Him. All I deserved from Jesus was His destruction. Yet He gave me the gift of being called not His slave, not His soldier, not His distant cousin who He only sees on occasion. No. He gave me the gift of the securest love in the world; I'm called His child. I have never doubted my parents' love, and now that I'm a mom, I know what it means to love a child. It's truly unconditional. There is nothing that would change my love for them; it's the most secure love we humans are capable of. It doesn't change, and God calls me His child. That should be enough to wake me up every morning filled with gratefulness and joy. I am His.

PRAYER

Lord, remind me when I forget just how miraculous it is to simply know You. But that's not where You left it. I don't just simply know You. You call me Yours, Your cherished child. Let this fact produce in me great joy!

....

....

....

....

....

....

....

....

....

....

....

....

continue your personal prayer

I NEED YOUR HELP, LORD!

My little children, let us not love in word or in tongue, but in deed and in truth. And by this we know that we are of the truth and shall assure our hearts before Him. For if our heart condemns us, God is greater than our heart, and knows all things. Beloved, if our heart does not condemn us, we have confidence toward God. And whatever we ask we receive from Him, because we keep His commandments and do those things that are pleasing in His sight. And this is His commandment: that we should believe on the name of His Son Jesus Christ and love one another, as He gave us commandment.
—1 John 3:18–23

I want to be holy. I want to reflect God's heart. I pray every day to be used by Him. I used to think I was something special, but the closer I get to my God, the more I realize just how messed up and far away from God's heart I am. I see it in my heart, in my speech, and at times in my actions. Everything about our lives are intertwined, but I would dare to say that the most important, or at least most obvious to those around us, is our speech.

> Out of the abundance of a man's heart the mouth speaks. (Luke 6:45b)

When we speak, it reveals our hearts. What we say is more important than I think we realize. Life and death are in the power of the tongue (Proverbs 18:21), which means we have, with our mouth, the power to demolish or to build. Have you ever looked up the definition of sarcasm?

> sarcasm: *noun*: the use of irony to mock or convey contempt.

> contempt: noun: the feeling that a person or a thing is beneath consideration, worthless, or deserving scorn.

Yes, sarcasm is, by definition, telling someone that you feel they are beneath you or worthless. This is the power of death coming out of our mouths and is usually used in the form of humor. How funny do you think it is to God when I demolish someone He died for with my words, in the name of humor? We can probably all think of a time when someone sarcastically said something that stung a little. A situation when walking away, we said to ourselves, "I know they were joking, but maybe they actually do feel that way about me. Maybe I am actually not worthy of respect in their sight."

My speech is more important than I realize. We have been given tremendous power with our words—to build up our brothers and sisters or to tear them down. The question is, am I going to choose to realize the power of my words or allow my heart to be hardened, saying, "It's only humor"?

PRAYER

Lord, let me take my words more seriously. Humor was created by You, and laughter is a gift from You, but sarcasm is not humor. Sarcasm is designed to hurt. Let me distinguish the difference, and let me choose to build up.

COVENANTAL RELATIONSHIP

There's something about marriage that powerfully emanates God's love so much clearer. Someone who knows you fully—all your cracks and shortcomings, no secrets, no deceptions, raw and fully you—still loves you deeply. Of course, we know God loves us unconditionally, which is different from any human capacity. The closest to unconditional love is good parents loving their children. Marriage is different in the sense that it is two people, with (hopefully) no familial ties, deciding to love each other. Someone who didn't have to love you pursued you, saw all your flaws, and still said, "I want you, through good and bad." It's such a clearer picture of the love of Jesus, which is of course the sole purpose for marriage, to be the picture of Christ and His church.

No matter our relationship status, we are called to emanate our love for each other the way Christ loves us. This is so much easier when loving someone outside your home. Think about it. Showing love, joy, and kindness to someone at church is easy. It's easy to put your best foot forward in a thirty-minute or even a few-hour interaction. It's far harder to show love, joy, patience, and kindness in all moments of every day that you spend with your spouse. Here lies the beautiful, refining fire that is marriage. Jesus uses our spouse in our lives to purify our relationship with Him. He uses this covenantal relationship to build in us characteristics that couldn't have been built had the only outside interactions been with people at church or work or school. Those people don't know you. Even a roommate doesn't know you as well as your spouse. That can be scary but beautifully vulnerable.

You might be saying, "Marriage is a joke. Marriages typically don't last." I don't deny the unbelievable pain surrounding marriage in our culture. Imperfect people make messes. My argument is if you marry a genuine believer in Christ Jesus, and you're a genuine believer, you both have the power dwelling inside you to overcome any obstacle. Will it be easy? Absolutely not. Will it be possible? Emphatically, I say yes!

Divorce is not a word we use in our home. Divorce is so incredibly painful because of the intimacy in which you have engaged. Someone who knew you fully, who you let in, now says, "I no longer want you." That was never the design of marriage. God hates divorce because it is an action so far from His character. God never makes a vow He won't keep. He vows to love you unconditionally, and He means it. God never lies. Divorce hurts. It doesn't just hurt the couple involved but anyone within a large radius. If you're the child of a broken family, I don't have to tell you how painful it is.

I've been blessed enough to be the child of two parents who stuck it out through thick and thin. They are the greatest example to me that marriage can last, even if it's hard at times. I am forever grateful for them choosing each other, and because of this, I have confidence that we can make it, and so can you. It just comes down to choice.

> Though one may be overpowered by another, two can withstand him. And a threefold cord is not quickly broken. (Ecclesiastes 4:12)

PRAYER

Lord, You are so good. You put the people, the trials, and the refinement exactly where it should be in my life. Let me cling tightly to You. Bless my marriage (or future marriage if you're not married yet). Let it be a blessing to me as well as a sweet aroma of Your love for Your church.

JESUS SAID, "WHO TOUCHED ME?"

And a woman was there who had been subject to
bleeding for twelve years, but no one could heal her.
She came up behind him and touched the edge of his
cloak, and immediately her bleeding stopped.
"Who touched me?" Jesus asked.
When they all denied it, Peter said, "Master, the
people are crowding and pressing against you."
But Jesus said, "Someone touched me; I know
that power has gone out from me."
Then the woman, seeing that she could not go unnoticed,
came trembling and fell at his feet. In the presence of
all the people, she told why she had touched him and
how she had been instantly healed. Then he said to her,
"Daughter, your faith has healed you. Go in peace."
—Luke 8:43–48

This woman was at her end, desperate. No doctor, no amount of money could heal her. She was a social outcast because of her condition.

Jesus is so capable of healing and changing her life. He doesn't even have to know He's doing it.

Our biggest problems, our worst conditions, our lost cause, what the doctors cannot fix—they are effortless for Jesus. Whatever we might be facing today, remember that Jesus healed this women without even being aware. All it took was her faith to believe He could and the power He has within Him.

PRAYER

Lord, let me understand Your greatness. I believe You can heal any condition. You can right any wrong. I trust You. I know You have a plan. I choose to believe. I choose to draw close.

....

....

....

....

....

....

....

....

....

....

....

continue your personal prayer

TO HEAR YOU
SAY THAT I'M
YOUR FRIEND

Draw me close to You. Never let me go. I'd lay it all down again. To hear You say that I'm Your friend. Help me find a way to bring me back to You. You're all I want. You're all I've ever needed. You're all I want. Help me know You are near. You are my desire. No one else will do. 'Cause nothing else could take Your place. To feel the warmth of Your embrace. Help me find a way to bring me back to You. You're all I want. You're all I've ever needed. You're all I want. Help me know You are near.
—"Draw Me Close to You" lyrics by Kutless

I've loved this song for a long time, but one day in church, the worship leader said something that made me love it even more. "Now we're going to sing this song again, but instead of singing it to God, think of it as He's singing it to you."

The only place I would disagree with the song being able to work in reverse is where it says, "You're all I've ever needed." What I would say is you're the reason He died. You're the only one He needed in order for Him to lay His life down on the cross. If it was just you, His work would have still been done. He powerfully loves us. I don't know if it's just me, but sometimes I wrongly think of Jesus as just tolerating me. I know He loves me, but maybe He's kind of annoyed by my constant fumbling of life. The truth is Jesus laid it all down. He would do it again just for me, just for you. He wants us. He desires my heart. When I'm going astray, He goes out and looks for me, as for that one lost sheep, saying, "Help me find a way to bring me back to you." He so desires to find us, but we also have to help Him into our hearts. It gave me chills to think of Jesus saying these verses to me. How much He desires for me to be close, to call Him my friend.

PRAYER

Lord, let this song be as true of my heart toward You as it of Your heart toward me.

....

....

....

....

....

....

....

....

....

....

....

continue your personal prayer

I HAD TO

And even as they did not like to retain God in *their* knowledge,
God gave them over to a debased mind, to do those things
which are not fitting; being filled with all unrighteousness,
sexual immorality, wickedness, covetousness, maliciousness;
full of envy, murder, strife, deceit, evil-mindedness; *they are*
whisperers, backbiters, haters of God, violent, proud, boasters,
inventors of evil things, disobedient to parents, undiscerning,
untrustworthy, unloving, unforgiving, unmerciful; who,
knowing the righteous judgment of God, that those who
practice such things are deserving of death, not only do
the same but also approve of those who practice them.
—Romans 1:28–32

I know I am not the only one who reads this and thinks it sounds
all too familiar.

"I pledge allegiance to the flag of the United States of America,
and to the republic for which it stands, one nation, under God,
indivisible, with liberty and justice for all."

This nation was founded on a God-fearing platform, but not
wanting to "retain God in our knowledge," He gave us over to a
debased, reprobate, or devalued mind. God will not be mocked.
Sure, we might still say this pledge, we might still sing "God bless
America" (although this action is starting to be called racist), and we
might still acknowledge the baby Jesus on Christmas and the cross
on Easter, but do we truly as a nation give God the glory for the
blessings we have here in the US? No. In fact, we have taken God
out of our schools, our politics, our country, and our lives as much

as we possibly can. Then we wonder why our political leaders can't seem to make logical decisions, why there's another school shooting every other week, why there are acts of pure evil daily, why there's so much immortality, so much murder, so much hate. We wonder why no one seems to have common sense anymore.

> The fear of God is the beginning of wisdom and the knowledge of the Holy One is understanding. (Proverbs 9:10)

My generation doesn't fear anyone—no teachers, police officers, judges, and especially not God. I'd say the generations before us are the ones to blame. The ones who decided to kick God out of our country. He has given us over to what we wanted. We are now paying the price. How do we feel, America? Feel like repenting yet?

PRAYER

Lord, we pray for our nation. We pray for the hearts and minds lost in confusion. Let us learn to fear You, for we know we will be blessed with wisdom when we do.

....

....

....

....

....

....

continue your personal prayer

I AM SUCH
A SINNER

The further I walk with Jesus, the more I see my heart so much further from His. The more I see the sin so much clearer, the more I realize my drastic need for a Savior.

This realization can take me one of two different ways. It can humble me on my face before the Lord, drawing me closer to His heart in my critical need of Him, or it can devastate and demobilize me. I can let it be used by God and for my growth and His glory, or for Satan and his cause to steal, kill, and destroy. It can be freeing in some powerful ways to realize our utter inability to live this life well without Jesus. To know I need Him in my every breath takes the pressure off of my performance.

We must fight the condemnation of the enemy with this realization. If we are already convinced that there is nothing good in us, that we can do nothing without Jesus, what other darts does the enemy have to shoot at us? Condemnation is his biggest weapon. We should never let him attack us with condemnation again but receive the conviction of the Holy Spirit to be changed into the image of our Savior.

But God be thanked that *though* you were slaves of sin, yet you obeyed from the heart that form of doctrine to which you were delivered. And having been set free from sin, you became slaves of righteousness. (Romans 6:17–18)

PRAYER

Lord, thank You that You provide truth to set us free from sin. The truth is You died because I cannot be righteous in myself. Let this truth set us free.

....

....

....

....

....

....

....

....

....

....

....

....

....

continue your personal prayer

FEELING WEARY?

Do you ever read and feel like you got nothing? So you feel like you should read again, but then you get distracted by all the other things that need to be done? That was me these past couple weeks, and as a result, I've felt strung out, stressed out, and emptied out.

I've heard it said, "If Satan can't make you bad, he'll make you busy."

I think that is so true. Lately, I feel like I'm running. Running from place to place, running to take care of my home, my husband and children, running and not finding rest in my Savior. Jesus was never in a hurry. He would always take time, as much as it took, to seek His father. Sometimes it would get interrupted or delayed, but we always see Him prioritizing that time. I want to be like this. Not that it's okay to be late anywhere, but if I have to be somewhere, I wake up with enough time to be renewed by my Father. Just like relationships with friends or family, if you don't spend deep, meaningful time with them, your relationship is going to be pretty superficial, but if you spend time actually talking about the deep, meaningful things in your life, you will have a deep relationship. Time spent is important. He gave it all for us. The least we can do is give Him some time.

Find a place today to spend ten minutes distraction-free with Jesus, listening to His voice, seeking His truth. You won't regret how it changes Your day.

But seek first the kingdom of God and His righteousness, and all these things shall be added to you. (Matthew 6:33)

PRAYER

Lord, let me seek Your face in this moment with a pure heart and genuine love. Renew my soul in this time.

....

....

....

....

....

....

....

....

....

....

....

continue your personal prayer

JESUS, THE CALMER OF MY SOUL

Things changed so much for me in 2017. I met my (now) husband in July, dated long-distance from Oregon and Texas, got engaged in October, married and shared our first kiss together on our wedding day in November, and found out we were pregnant with our first baby in February 2018. We had our first baby three weeks before our first wedding anniversary, our second baby in July 2020, and our third baby in August 2022. We have moved ten times in three different states in the last seven years. Needless to say, in all of that, there has been stress, strife, and struggle at times. Insane amounts of growth happened in those first few years of marriage and parenthood. As a twenty-one-year-old, I don't think I realized just how selfish and immature I was until I had a baby of my own. I was stretched, heated, hammered, and refined more than I ever thought possible in those first few years. I felt so overwhelmed with marriage, moving, and motherhood, along with the sleeplessness that accompanied my oldest child for his first year and a half of life. There were moments I didn't think I would make it.

But I'm here to say Jesus is faithful! The old saying is true; what doesn't kill us makes us stronger. But I would take it a step further and say, "What doesn't kill us today solidifies our faith and sanctifies our tomorrow."

Though I didn't feel it was grace at the time, it was the grace of Jesus putting me through so many trials, simply because He knew when I came out on the other side, I'd possess tools and characteristics that I needed to be blessed. I am able to see the true, intense growth from that very hard season of life. During a sleepless night (because yes, they still frequently happen with three toddlers), I'm less prone to get angry as I once did. During the middle of a toddler meltdown, I'm not as embarrassed or anxious. If a nap is disrupted, I don't view it as a catastrophe, which was my typical reaction. When I tell you I was an anxious mess as a first-time mom, I mean it was like pulling teeth to get me to leave the house with my baby, and if I did happen to leave, I would internally panic if I was out and my baby was missing nap time.

It's actually so humorous to look back on just how out of my mind I was. My poor husband probably thought he married a psycho, but that was my trial. I had to grow through it, and I'm so thankful now for that test. I'll continue to face trials so long as I live, and they more than likely won't ever be fun, but being on the other side of this one gives me the ability to know that I can get through. Jesus can and will use it for my good and His glory.

Maybe you're going through something hard right now, overwhelming even. As hard as it may be, take joy and lean into Jesus. He is the calmer of our soul, the comfort and strength of our life. You will come out of this fire stronger than you were before.

Be still and know that I am God. (Psalm 46:10)

PRAYER

Lord, I'm thankful for the struggles and the trials, as they only give me fortitude, strength in faith, and the ability to declare Your faithfulness and sovereignty over our lives.

....

....

continue your personal prayer

SIN IS FUN ONLY FOR A SEASON (A MESSAGE TO THE YOUNGER ME)

Oh stubborn, rebellious, foolish young girl. You knew the truth. You knew your parents were loving and protecting you, yet you did not listen. You planted seeds of sin, and you reap the consequences every day. You deal with the pain that rebellion caused in your life. You struggle to lay down your constant shame, the never-ending lies of the wicked one, at the feet of Jesus daily. If you had just listened, if you had just obeyed, it would all be different.

I thank God we have a Savior who is in the business of mending broken things, but there comes a point when you think, *Shouldn't I be mended? Shouldn't my heart not hurt so much by now?*

I have a message for all girls who are going through the phase of life that causes a crossroads, a time when you're figuring out who you are and what you believe. I made some life-altering mistakes during the ages of seventeen to nineteen years old. During this time of life, I was lost, I was insecure, and I was weak in my faith and lacked conviction. I have always had a rebellious spirit. I have always struggled to obey. I've believed the oldest lie, the one that deceived even Eve, that "God is holding out on you."

First of all, do not seek to please people. People will always fail. People always have the capacity to hurt you. Always be quick to forgive, but don't put your faith or your identity in what people think of you.

Second, *boys* are never worth it. I italicized boys because *boys* are the immature, narcissistic opposite gender. They come in all ages, shapes, and sizes, and they only have one thing on their mind. Our culture has made their agenda very apparent to all of us. No, girls! You're worth so much more! Stay away from boys!

A man who loves God, who knows His character and desires to live that character out! If he knows God and loves God, He will be a man who is honest, kind, patient, and forgiving and adores you and only you! This is who you want. Don't waste your time with anything else. You are precious in the sight of Jesus. You are fearfully and wonderfully made (Psalm 139:14). *Boys* are not only a waste of your time, but they are a detriment to your soul, identity, and self-worth. That might sound dramatic, but I promise you it's not. I deal every single day with the enemy's lies, ones that said, "That *boy* treated you exactly how you deserved, because you're worthless." That's a lie, lady, but it's one Satan can use against me because I allowed a sinful relationship to enter my life. Don't do it. Please!

Lastly, and the best news of all, there is hope! If you've made mistakes, Jesus still adores you. He loves you so much that He died for you! In the middle of your worst sin, when you were at your lowest, He looked at you and said, "This one's worth dying for!" Can we just let that sink in for a second? I feel like we hear it so much it loses its power.

Think of it this way. You do something terrible. You lawfully deserve death, and there's this person who loves you, who tried to talk to you all the time, but you just kept ignoring them, kept rejecting their love. Now you're awaiting your death for this terrible thing you've done, and this person steps out of the crowd and says, "I know she deserves death, but instead of her, take Me. I'll die in her place, because I've loved her so much, for so long."

This is what Jesus did for us. He not only died but beat death and rose again. He loves you, He loves me, and although we may still deal with the pain and scars of the past, we have all the hope we ever needed because of His undying love. He continues to heal my scars, but oh how much easier it would have been had I not made those decisions, had I been able to read this from my future self. Maybe I would have made different choices. Don't make the mistakes I did. Love God and hold fast to His life-giving commandments!

> *Let* love *be* without hypocrisy. Abhor what is evil. Cling to what is good. (Romans 12:9)

> Do not quench the Spirit. Do not despise prophecies. Test all things; hold fast what is good. Abstain from every form of evil. Now may the God of peace Himself sanctify you completely; and may your whole spirit, soul, and body be preserved blameless at the coming of our Lord Jesus Christ. (1 Thessalonians 5:19–23)

PRAYER

Lord, I pray Your spirit will fill my heart and discern my choices. Let me be wise.

....

....

....

....

....

....

....

continue your personal prayer

MY CHALLENGE—
LOVE LIKE CHRIST

For the love of Christ compels us, because we judge thus:
that if One died for all, then all died; and He died for all,
that those who live should live no longer for themselves,
but for Him who died for them and rose again.
Therefore, from now on, we regard no one according to
the flesh. Even though we have known Christ according
to the flesh, yet now we know *Him thus* no longer.
—2 Corinthians 5:14–16

Christ died for all. What if I went throughout my days seeing people for who they will be after Christ's work is done in them, rather than who they are right now? What if I chose to encourage them in who they'll be in Jesus in two, four, or ten years from now? What if I chose to see where they'll be when Christ's perfect work is finished in them, when they're robed in His righteousness? I can be quick to cut people down for their earthly flaws. This must not be so. Christ died for me and my many flaws in the exact same way and for the exact same reason He died for you! I believe if all of us Christians took up the challenge to see people how Jesus sees them, through His sanctified blood, this world would be a very different place!

PRAYER

Lord, show me Your heart for all. Let me love the way You do. Let me see the potential in all, and let me be an encourager. Let me speak life to everyone.

....

....

....

....

....

....

....

....

....

....

....

....

....

continue your personal prayer

FROM THE BEGINNING, HE CHOSE YOU

But we are bound to give thanks to God always for you,
brethren beloved by the Lord, because God from the beginning
chose you for salvation through sanctification by the Spirit
and belief in the truth, to which He called you by our gospel,
for the obtaining of the glory of our Lord Jesus Christ.
—2 Thessalonians 2:13–14

"From the beginning, He chose you." He chose me. And if you're in Him, or you want to be in Him, He chose you too! There's a lot of debate between people a lot smarter than me about predestination, or whether we choose Him or He chooses us. The way it makes sense in my simple mind is backed up in Romans, chapter 3, where it says, "There is no one righteous, no one who seeks Jesus." *But the Bible says we have to choose the gift of salvation*, you might be thinking. "If no one seeks after God, how do we choose Him?" The very act of us choosing Jesus and being saved is a miracle in and of itself. Jesus must put this desire into our hearts, and by doing so, He chooses us in order for us to choose Him. How incredible is that? He didn't have to choose me. I'm nothing special. There are far better, far braver, far more honorable people out there, but He chose me. I believe if I woke up every day with this reminder in my head, I would be far more motivated to love God and others better. I was chosen for no other reason than because of love, and to show this love is a no-brainer.

PRAYER

Lord, can You just help me grasp this blessing that You have given to me? You, the God of the universe, looked at me from the beginning, knowing all that I have done and ever will do—being unfaithful to you, profaning your name, dragging you through the pig pen with me—and somehow you still chose me. Oh, how I don't deserve it, yet I still somehow take it for granted. I don't even think about it most of the time, but there are people out there in this world right now with no hope. No hope at all. For them, this life is just empty and void. Life means nothing, and this is as good as it gets. Somehow, You, Jesus Christ, chose to reveal yourself to me. Lord, I thank You for giving me Your hope! Help me to never take it for granted. Help me to remember not everyone has it, but they can. Help me to be a tool in Your hands to pass this hope on.

....

....

....

....

....

....

....

....

continue your personal prayer

BE OF GOOD CHEER

But as for you, brethren, do not
grow weary in doing good.
—2 Thessalonians 3:13

This is a true challenge. Sometimes you feel like you're serving and getting nothing in return, or not even being treated fairly. It can be hard to continue with a cheerful heart. This morning, I was praying about some things I am dealing with in my own heart and life, and God reminded me of this verse, saying, "All My rewards for you are being stored up in heaven. Who cares about what you receive on earth?"

Easier read than learned, of course, but it's true. Who cares how people treat me or if they recognize my qualifications or how much experience I've had in a certain area. God will reward me for being humble. God will reward me for the character I have, the love I show, the joy I have in service to Him. I must say I have been failing lately. My attitude may be hiding it, but my heart feels a lot of weariness in service. This was a great reminder in this verse this morning to store up all my treasures in heaven, being focused on where I'll spend eternity instead of the silly, short-lived pats on the back here on earth. Whatever you may be dealing with today, be of good cheer! God sees the good you do even if no one else does! Even if no one appreciates you, God's rewards are better than any human accolades. This in itself should help us be joyful.

PRAYER

Lord, let everything I do be done as unto You. Let me not seek the approval or appreciation of people. Let me be content in pleasing You with my life and heart.

....

....

....

....

....

....

....

....

....

....

....

....

....

continue your personal prayer

I HAVE SO FAR TO GO, SO FAR TO GROW

Lately, I have just been listening to myself talk and then shaking my head in disbelief as to what just came out of my mouth. The theme of this week's prayers has been to tame my tongue. I'd like to think, at six months pregnant, that it's baby brain, that my hormones are controlling my mouth and my attitude. Yeah, I guess I could blame it on the baby. I know hormones do play a part, but it's really just my sin nature. I need God to daily sanctify me from myself.

The other day, I was talking with a family member, and we got on the subject of filthy language and how it pertains to the Christian life. I pointed out, "It says in the Bible that filthy language is not to even be named among the body of Christ." I couldn't recall where it says it, but I knew it did. This morning, I looked it up. You know what else it says in there? Do not slander (James 4:11), nor foolish talk nor course jesting (which means either joking crudely or with sarcasm) (Ephesians 5:4).

Hmm … see, I may not struggle very much with using cuss words, so it's easy for me to point out where the Bible might talk about this issue and how it shouldn't be a part of our lives as Christians, but I fail to point out issues that, even though I hate these actions, I still struggle with them in my own life. Ladies and gentlemen, it keeps becoming more and more apparent to me that if God can save and sanctify a hypocrite like me, He truly can save and sanctify anyone! Be encouraged today that we are all a work in progress, and just because we mess up, He's not finished with us!

PRAYER

Thank You for Your continued work in my life. Thank You for not leaving me where You found me. I can be certain You will always be working on me until I enter Your kingdom!

....

....

....

....

....

....

....

....

....

....

....

....

....

continue your personal prayer

GOD'S WORD
IS POWER

I was recently pondering a question. How many books have I read in my lifetime?

Probably not as many as some people but quite a few. Then I thought, *How many times have I read through the entire Bible cover to cover?* Well, probably not as many times as I read the Hunger Games series as a teenager. How sad that is! Why does it seem so hard to read the Bible? I can read any other book for hours on end, but if I tried to read the Bible for hours, I would be so exhausted. But why is that? Is it because there are so many hard words? Well, yes, there are some names in there that even some language professors might have to sound out, but for the most part, the Bible is pretty easy to read and understand. Is it because there are life truths that we can't grasp right away, and we need time to let them soak in? Yes, there are definitely deep and layered things we need time to ponder. But I would suggest that the main reason we find it so exhausting, so hard, is spiritual. Satan, the enemy of our souls, knows there is power in that book, power to defeat him and the darkness he brings. So he and his little minions are going to do their best to keep us out of it! They do this through questions that appeal to our flesh. "Aren't you tired? Don't you have to get up early? You should probably go to sleep; that would be the wise thing to do so you're not tired at work tomorrow. That's what God would want from you." Or "Don't you need to get other things done today? You don't have time to sit and pray!" But if you are doing any other activity, reading any other book, or watching any other movie, "Man, you don't need sleep! You can sleep when you're dead!" "You can binge-watch the whole series! Get your stuff done later!" Satan is crafty, so we have to be craftier! Always on guard and always fighting against him through the Word of God! For the Word of God is the power to defeat darkness, the strength we need to get through the day with joy, the only sustenance that will truly fulfill our soul.

> For man does not live by bread alone but by every word
> that proceeds from the mouth of God. (Matthew 4:4)

PRAYER

Lord, give me a hunger for Your Word. Block the enemy's schemes trying to keep me from Your Word, which brings life.

....

....

....

....

....

....

....

....

continue your personal prayer

GOD IS GOOD, JUST BECAUSE

Ever since I found out about our baby boy, I have been both excited and afraid. I'm excited to meet him but afraid that something might happen to him. I know that is probably just called "being a parent." But this morning, the Lord convicted and revealed to me why this fear has such a hold on me.

I subconsciously believe that God rewards us for the good we do, but for the bad we've done, he passively punishes us. I wrongly picture Him with one eyebrow raised and arms crossed, just kind of sitting back with a disappointed scowl, saying, "I told you not to do that. Now I guess you'll see why." Although consequences to our actions do happen, it actually breaks God's heart when He sees us hurting. He's not irritated. He's weeping with us, saying, "I wish it didn't have to be like this."

For some reason, I have had a hard time believing that God will be good to me because of all the bad I've been to Him. I brace myself for a heartbreak to come. I fear every day that I will get a call that a loved one has died. I am anxious about my husband traveling every week down windy roads, but the greatest fear of all is that something will happen to my unborn baby, or worse, to him after he is born. Now, this isn't a fear I have been fully aware of. It has always been in the back of my mind. But as I was praying this morning, God revealed that I don't fully trust and believe that He is good just because. I'm believing the lie that somehow I have to do and be better for Him to bless me. I have to earn His protection and that I can earn His favor. I am so thankful that is not the case. I'm so grateful His grace is the only reason I am here today and the only reason I will be in heaven when I leave this earth. I need to repent of my unbelief and trust that He has me and my family in His loving hands, that His plans are always the best and His mercy never fails (Lamentations 3:22). I need to trust that He is good.

> *Through* the Lord's mercies we are not consumed,
> Because His compassions fail not. *They are* new every morning;
> Great *is* Your faithfulness. "The Lord *is* my portion,"
> says my soul,
> "Therefore I hope in Him!" (Lamentations 3:22–24)

PRAYER

Lord, let me trust that Your plans are always best. Let me trust that no matter what I face in this life, I face it with Your power on my side. With You, I can get through anything.

....

....

....

....

....

....

....

continue your personal prayer

REALITY SMACK

My brethren, count it all joy when you fall into various
trials, knowing that the testing of your faith produces
patience. But let patience have *its* perfect work, that you
may be perfect and complete, lacking nothing.
—James 1:2–4

Last night after having kind of a hard evening, I came home
talking to Chad. "All I want to do is help, but when people have
bad attitudes, it makes me want to just leave. It's like, man, if they
don't appreciate what I'm trying to do, then why do I even bother?"
I ranted

"That's not really the attitude you want to have," my wise
husband said to me.

In that second, I heard the Lord whisper to me, "My child, now
you get a taste of what I have gone through, with you and for you.
Rejected, spit on, or metaphorical eyes rolled at on a daily basis, I
still patiently love."

"Oh … yeah." Reality smacks me in the face again! In light
of what Jesus did and does for me daily, why can't I show patient
love to someone else who needs it? To count it all joy because
God somehow counts me worthy to continue working on my
heart. To remember that every trial I face, big or small, is actually
incredible because it gives me the chance, if I let it, to make me
stronger in my walk with the Lord and to produce in me heavenly
character. I become so much more aware every day of the sinner
I am! I need Jesus, and I'm so thankful that I have Him! I also

couldn't be more thankful for the beautiful, undeserved blessings He has given me.

PRAYER

Lord, let me remember all that You've done for me, how You love me no matter what. I can extend that same love to others.

....

....

....

....

....

....

....

....

....

....

....

continue your personal prayer

A LESSON IN TRUST

Trust in the Lord with all your heart,
And lean not on your own understanding;
In all your ways acknowledge Him,
And He shall direct your paths.
—Proverbs 3:5–6

My entire first pregnancy, I was filled with fear! Instead of giving my fear to my Lord, I held onto it, expecting the worst. You see, I didn't fully trust the Lord. I didn't fully trust that He was good, that His plans are perfect. *Surely, I don't deserve God's blessings; I deserve His punishment.* Knowing this, I expected to receive His correction through my child's well-being. I spent almost ten months worrying about my baby. When the day came to finally have him, instead of trusting my Lord and placing my life restfully in His hands, I was just terrified that something might happen to my baby.

We cannot deny that bad and hard things do happen in this life, none of which had a place in God's plan. Pain, sickness, heartbreak, death ... none of it was within God's perfect plan. We were never originally created to face any of these things, which is why they're so painful and impossible to understand. Sin entered this world and with it every kind of brokenness. God doesn't want us to sin because when we engage with those actions, brokenness, like a ravenous lion, is released in our life to devour us. But make no mistake. God does not wish these things upon us. He can and will use these things within our lives for our good and His glory.

Reading Romans 9 about vessels of mercy and vessels of wrath, I am reminded that it is only because of His grace that I am even here, that I am healthy, that He loves me and died for me. If I continue to expect His payback for the evil I have committed, I am essentially saying that, because my bad choices and mistakes deserve his punishment and because I will inevitably receive said punishment, my good actions could somehow also earn His grace. How could this be? There is none righteous, no not one; there is none who understands; there is none who seek after God (Romans 3:10–11). So then, if I am evil in and of myself, and He is the only good in me, then His grace is not earned by the good I have done, nor is His wrath earned by the bad I have done. If that were the case, I'd surely end up in hell. Our God is trustworthy, gracious, and worthy of all of our praise! He loves you and me more than we could ever fathom! We do not have to fear. We can trust Him in any and all situations.

PRAYER

Lord, You are so good! You are so worthy of praise. Please help me trust You with all of my heart. Reveal yourself to me just a little deeper today, I pray.

....

....

....

....

....

continue your personal prayer

LEARNING WHILE WATCHING

Being a mom has revealed a whole new kind of love—an overwhelming, overflowing love that I can't even begin to explain. It has given me a glimpse of the love that God has for us, only He loves us perfectly! I have to admit there are those regretful times, especially in the middle of the night, when I've gotten up for the tenth time to put him back to sleep, and the thoughts come that are *not* the perfect form of love. But God loves us perfectly, even when we are in the dark of night, feeling alone and screaming at the top of our lungs for Him to feed us, screaming so loudly that we can't even hear Him say, "Buddy, it's okay. Just one second. Be patient. I will be there. I'll feed you." Maybe those times I can't hear Him is when I'm crying too loudly. I say, "No, I want satisfaction to my discomfort now! I don't want to wait for You." So we cry and cry and cry, stuck in our beds because we cannot do anything on our own. Sure, we can kick and swing our arms around, smacking ourselves in the face, close our eyes and scream, not realizing that it is our own hand that is scratching our own faces. Yes, I've learned a lot about myself watching my son. But even in five weeks, I've seen so much growth. He's learned that when I say his name, I'm close. I'm about to get him out of his bed, about to satisfy his hunger, about to give him what he needs. He still has only a few seconds of patience, but he's learning. The longer we spend in the presence of our loving Father, the more we will learn about Him, and the more we will grow patient, knowing He is there, He is faithful, He will get us out, He will feed us, and He will snuggle us, rock us, change us, and love us. We will stop kicking in anger and smacking ourselves in the face. Will we still have times of throwing fits and doubting? Sure we will, but as we grow and mature, we will learn that the fits get us nowhere faster, that He is always there, and that He provides for us in the perfect time.

PRAYER

Lord, I pray that I will know You as my comforter! You are my sustainer of life. You hold me in Your arms. I am precious in Your sight!

....

....

....

....

....

....

....

....

....

....

continue your personal prayer

I WAS SUCH A BETTER MOM BEFORE I HAD A BABY

I was such a better mom before I had a baby. Meaning, my thoughts of how I would do things, the ideas of how easy it would be all fell out the window when I became an actual mom. I have been humbled beyond belief. No surprise, it's actually a lot harder than I expected.

Ever since I was little, all I wanted was to be a momma. At four and five years old, I would carry around my baby dolls. When I got a little older and my little brother came along, I would pretend I was his mommy, carrying him around and rocking him to sleep. Being a pretend mom was so easy. From the moment I found out I was pregnant with my first, I dreamed about holding my little baby. I believed it would be pure bliss, that the love I would feel for him would overshadow any hard times. I would just float around on cloud nine with my precious little one. I'd watch him sleep and just love every second of his life.

Then came my munchkin. Don't get me wrong. I love him more than life itself, but he is a tiny sinner holding a mirror to show me the ugly sin in my own heart. It is definitely not the airy, fairy marshmallows on popsicle sticks that I thought it would be. He has been a challenge from day one. We do have our giggles and our sweet cuddles, but he is a real person with a real personality and real and loud emotions. I believe he is a hammer and chisel in the hands of my Savior. God has done, and is doing, some serious demolition of the selfish heart I have had my whole life. I never realized just how selfish I was until that sweet baby came. I have spent a lot of time angry before the Lord, asking Him why He gave me such a discontent, sleepless child for my first baby, asking Him if I was only supposed to have one baby or what!

I received the answer, "No. You're supposed to change." He has shown me the areas in my heart that are all about me. I realized the times that I get most frustrated with Brim is when he messes up my time. My sleep, my workout, my quiet time—my pre baby, scheduled, and easily compartmentalized life. Every part of my life up until the moment I held that baby for the first time was truly all about me. Now God is changing who I put first. Slowly, I am recognizing my depravity in a serious way. Without my son, I would not have seen it. Children are such a blessing! They give us an opportunity every day to become more Christlike. That's not easy or always enjoyable, but a blessing it truly is! I need my Savior in a new and greater way just to get through each day. I thank God for my baby, who keeps me on my knees and running to my Lord for strength! No matter what stage of life we're in, we can thank God for the struggles that are bringing us one step closer to godliness!

> My brethren, count it all joy when you fall into various trials, knowing that the testing of your faith produces patience. But let patience have *its* perfect work, that you may be perfect and complete, lacking nothing. (James 1:2–4)

PRAYER

Lord, I thank You for the struggles, for the refining fire purifying my heart. Continue Your work in my life.

continue your personal prayer

FINDING GRACE
IN THE MIDDLE
OF THE NIGHT

My baby boy doesn't sleep. Usually, he wakes up in the middle of the night, stays awake for one to two hours, and then wakes again at 5:00 a.m. I am exhausted, and I have spent almost eight months angry at God. My husband and I pray nightly that God will help him sleep so that we all can rest, and every so often, we will get a night or even a week of nights that he sleeps, but for the last two months, we have been battling seemingly endless sleepless nights. Last night, after sitting by my son's crib for two hours while he screamed, I had a mental and emotional breakdown. I went out to the living room, pressed my face down into the couch, and screamed. Then I just started sobbing. "Don't You care that we are all suffering from exhaustion? Why won't You help? James talks about asking for wisdom without doubting, and it will be given. I'm not doubting that You can help me, that You can give me wisdom, but still You don't. Why not?" (Sleeplessness makes me a little more dramatic.)

"Baylee," my heavenly Father whispered, "you don't see it, but I'm building in you character that you cannot ·receive any other way. You have been so used to living life for yourself, doing whatever you want whenever you want. Now you have to live selflessly, and there is no other way to learn to be selfless than to be forced to do it. I am using your son to sand off those rough edges so that you can be smooth and ready for the future trials you will face. Ultimately, it will all be for a purpose, for everything I work together for the good of those who love Me and are called according to My purpose (Romans 8:28). Everything is for a season; it will not last forever (Ecclesiastes 3:1–8). No tribulations are endured in vain. Consider them pure joy (James 1:2–4)." I realized something as soon as He was finished speaking: we serve an awesome and merciful God. Who do I think I am that I deserve anything good from Him? What have I ever done to deserve His favor? Yet still He speaks so softly, so gracefully to an angry, ungrateful daughter. I could be facing so many worse things than sleeplessness, but I'm not. We're all healthy, we have a home to live in, family who loves us, friends to enjoy life with, and most of all a God who adores us infinitely. I am so blessed in this life, yet I still talk to God like I deserve something more. I am just so glad He is who He is. He's so gracious and merciful.

I have been living in shame. I don't feel adequate for this motherhood job. I feel like I'm failing because I can't figure out how to help this baby sleep. I'm losing my temper way too often out of pure exhaustion. I feel like my whole personality has changed, and I can't even think. I lose track of my words midsentence and most of the time feel awkward and brainless. I can't find time to actually focus on the Lord, because either I fall asleep reading His Word or my son wakes in the middle of my Bible study. By the time I get him back to sleep, it's time to do chores. But one thing I realized last night is, yes, I may be running around like Martha, but one thing I'm lacking is sitting at the feet of Jesus like Mary. That doesn't necessarily mean sitting. My baby just started crawling, and I fear I will *never* sit again. But sitting at the feet of Jesus is not always a physical posture; sometimes it is a spiritual posture—choosing to look at the struggle as pure joy, setting my heart in His hands, and trusting in His plan. Praising Him that He cares enough to change me! He loves me enough to allow struggle in my life so that I don't grow complacent, so that I keep fighting to know Him and to be like Him.

PRAYER

I praise You, God, for what You are working in my life, and I choose to look at it as joy from here on out. Help me walk in this revelation. Keep me in Your loving arms.

....

....

....

....

....

....

....

....

....

....

....

....

....

continue your personal prayer

CLINGING TIGHTLY

This morning, I was playing with my son. His favorite game lately has been to hand you an object and then take it back, so we were playing that game. Pretty soon, he grabbed my phone and handed it to me, but knowing he's not supposed to play with my phone, he made sure and kept a strong grip on it when he handed it to me. He wanted to make sure I would give it back. He never fully let go because he knew he probably wouldn't get it back. He's so happy to play this game with a ball or a stuffed animal or any toy that he knows he's allowed to play with, but the moment he gets his hands on something that's not a toy or maybe even something dangerous, such as toxic cleaners or knives out of the dishwasher or anything he knows I will take away from him, he holds on so much tighter, and he usually fusses when they're taken away.

Isn't this how I am so often when I hand things to the Lord? I hand things up but never fully surrender it, because He might take it and never give it back. So often, I want something in life that God knows is not beneficial or maybe even destructive to my life. When He asks me to hand it over, I do, but I hold on with a tight grip, hoping He will give it back. Being the loving Father He is, sometimes He has to use force to take things away. I don't take things away from my son because I want to squash his fun or make his life miserable. I love him. I love to see him happy and having fun, but because I love him, I take things away because it's not beneficial or it's dangerous.

Being a parent definitely sheds a whole new light on the character of our loving Father.

"All things are lawful unto me," but all things are not expedient. "All things are lawful for me," but I will not be brought under the power of any. (1 Corinthians 6:12)

The Lord is my strength and my shield; my heart trusts in him, and he helps me. My heart leaps for Joy, with my song I praise him. (Psalm 28:7–9)

PRAYER

Lord, let me live this life in full surrender to You. Let me open my hands and completely let go whenever I'm tempted to hold on tight.

....

....

....

....

....

....

....

....

continue your personal prayer

SEASON OF DOUBT

Have you ever gone through a season of self-doubt? I'm in that season now, a season of finding my new identity in Christ as a young wife and mom. I feel like there was a point when I found myself confident in who I was in Christ as just a single woman. I look back on that season with fond memories, a time when, for possibly the first time in my life, I liked who I was because I really felt like I knew my purpose in Jesus, and I was given a platform in Mexico, as a missionary, to proclaim Him.

Now I'm a wife and mom. I love this job, but I'm insecure in it. I second-guess all the time if I'm doing a good job raising my son, if I'm being a good example, if I'm being a good wife and balancing those roles well. That insecurity seems to spill over into all my other relationships as well. Insecurity mixes with sleeplessness, and I seem to second-guess everything. In all that second-guessing, I'm more and more aware of my failings. Most of the time, I don't like myself or the way I interact with my family and friends. I've asked the Lord in prayer what I need to do to get out of this insecurity rut I've been in since the birth of my son, and this scripture jumped in my head: "seek first the kingdom of God and His righteousness and all these other things will be added to you" (Matthew 6:33).

Of course, this made me evaluate the question "What I have been seeking first?" The answer is I've been seeking to do it all in my own power, to muster up the strength to be a righteous, loving, generous wife, mom, and friend, all on my own. Of course I'd be insecure. I can't do anything good in my own strength. The beginning of this section in Matthew 6 is talking about worry, and essentially, insecurity is worry. I'm worried about what my family or other people around me will think. It's pointless, but I cannot fight these insecurities without seeking first the kingdom of God. This is the key element that I feel has been lacking since my son was born. So many more distractions have been added to our life, but it is so much more important than ever to find the time to armor my every day with the truth. I know I will never be perfect, but I want so much to be grounded in His truth day after day.

PRAYER

Lord, I'm so thankful to not be lost anymore but found by You! I am deeply loved by the creator of this world, Jesus Christ, my Lord. Let every day be grounded in You.

....

....

....

....

....

....

....

....

....

continue your personal prayer

OBEDIENCE IS BETTER

Being a mom has been the most rewarding and the most disheartening experience of my life. I have come to realize that the discipline and level of obedience I establish in my child in his early years will have a major eternal effect on his life and heart in the future as it relates to God and his obedience to Him.

There are so many times I find myself so humbled and thankful for the sweet, smart child the Lord has blessed me with. Other times, I find myself asking why I got such a smart, stubborn child for my first one. "I could've used an easier practice, God!"

So often, I am greatly reminded of spiritual truths while watching my son grow and learn every day. He watches me, and if he feels he can get away with something, he will attempt it. A lot of times, he feels that the things I tell him not to do are things that are just too fun for me to let him enjoy. The reality is that a lot of the things I tell him not to do are actually for his own good. He quickly realizes this fact when he touches something hot that I've told him not to touch and gets burned, or if he drops something on his foot that I told him not to pick up.

Isn't that just like us in our spiritual life? So often, God clearly states in His Word things we are to avoid, and yet, just like Eve, we believe the lie, that He is trying to keep us from all the fun. I know often, like my child, I have had to get burned and learn the hard way why our good, good Father tells us not to do this or that. It's not to crush our fun but to protect our hearts. There is so much of a tendency to think, *I am the exception; this won't hurt me the way it did them.* But trust me, sin hurts much worse than a burn on the hand or a bruise on the foot, and it's so much better to just be obedient rather than have to face the consequences and pick up the pieces of a broken heart. Following God's commands will protect you from all pain. Obedience might be hard, but it is the better choice.

> The fear of the Lord is clean, enduring forever; The judgements of the Lord are true and righteous all together. (Psalm 19:9)

PRAYER

Lord, let me fight my sin nature and trust Your promises—trust that You are good, You want what's best for me, and so Your warnings are to be heeded.

....

....

....

....

....

....

....

....

....

continue your personal prayer

YOU WILL DIE. NOW HOW WILL YOU LIVE?

(Today's daily reading was written at the very start of COVID. We still had no idea what was happening. Little did I know at the time of writing this the insanity wouldn't end; there has never been a going back to normal. With that said, I chose to leave this in the book because I believe everything written here can still be applied to today.)

While doing what I'm pretty sure the rest of the nation, and maybe even the world, was doing, listening up on the latest news, I began to feel very anxious. I have a precious little life I'm responsible for, and I'm about to bring another new little life into this world in just a few short months. What kind of world are my kids going to grow up in? What's the future going to look like? What's the economic state going to be? Will we even be able to make ends meet? Will our small business crash? What will we do? All the questions come flooding to my brain, when suddenly I was totally convicted by such a simple piece of scripture. "Do not worry about your life" (Matthew 6:25a).

We as Christians speak so freely about the hope we have in Jesus. It's so easy to speak this way when things in our life are going well. But people are watching us to see how we are going to react through the storms. Will we retain the peace, or will we panic? We have the whole story; we know how it turns out, where this world ultimately ends up. Our hope, our peace in knowing this world is not our home, while everyone is panicking, should be what stops people in their tracks. It should bring the question, "What do they have that I don't?"

I mean, let's think about it for a moment. Say this pandemic really is going to kill us all. Will panicking help? Will it help us spread the hope of Jesus if we're just as scared as everyone else? What if we do get sick and die? Don't we believe that our last breath on earth is our first breath in heaven? Don't get me wrong. I don't want to die any more than the next person. My point is our eternal state is a lot more important than here in the temporal. We're all going to die! All of us will taste death, unless Jesus comes to get us. Don't we want as many people as possible to come with us to eternal bliss? Our reaction to this chaos matters more than I think we realize. It's easy to fall into the panic. But knowing what the Word says about worry can help us realize just how silly it is. He's got us. He knows what we need. He's a loving Father and a faithful supplier of our needs. Trust and believe.

> "Therefore I say to you, do not worry about your life, what you will eat or what you will drink; nor about your body, what you will put on. Is not life more than food and the body more than clothing? Look at the birds of the air, for they neither sow nor reap nor gather into barns; yet your heavenly Father feeds them. Are you not of more value than they? Which of you by worrying can add one cubit to his stature?

> "So why do you worry about clothing? Consider the lilies of the field, how they grow: they neither toil nor spin; and yet I say to you that even Solomon in all his glory was not arrayed like one of these. Now if God so clothes the grass of the field, which today is, and tomorrow is thrown into the oven, *will He* not much more *clothe* you, O you of little faith?"

> "Therefore do not worry, saying, 'What shall we eat?' or 'What shall we drink?' or 'What shall we wear?' For after all these things the Gentiles seek. For your heavenly Father knows that you need all

these things. But seek first the kingdom of God and His righteousness, and all these things shall be added to you. Therefore do not worry about tomorrow, for tomorrow will worry about its own things. Sufficient for the day *is* its own trouble. (Matthew 6:25–34)

PRAYER

Lord, let me not worry. Let me trust in You with all my heart and lean on You and not on my own understanding.

....

....

....

....

....

....

....

....

....

....

continue your personal prayer

MOTHERHOOD
IN A WORD

Motherhood in a word— Refining.
Although the journey is beautiful and full of joyous times, two years ago, I never would have expected so many struggles.

The newborn stage is tough—endless days with wakings that never seem spaced out quite enough, feeling like I couldn't possibly make it even one more minute without sleep.

We prayed our entire second pregnancy that we would have an easier baby, one who simply liked to sleep. "Babies that like to sleep do exist! Other people have them. Why can't we?" After six weeks of never getting more than three consecutive hours of sleep on a really good night, I woke up just a little on the wrong side of the bed this morning. We woke at eight, nine, twelve, one, three, four, and five and finally gave up at six thirty this morning. When I started to complain, I heard this: "I am not a genie in a bottle. I don't just show up to grant your wish. I love you too much to do that. Instead, I want to build in you character that will last for eternity, character that can only be produced through struggle. Choose joy, for I am working in your life."

I don't know who else needs to hear this, but I certainly did. Sometimes I get so stuck on my struggles here on earth I forget what He has already done for me. I'm going to heaven because He loves me. He loves me for no other reason than because He wants to! I can't earn it! I'm a dirty, rotten sinner. Having two tough children magnifies and shows me this daily! I need Him! The more I focus on the character He's producing in me for eternity, the easier the trial seems! I am so thankful for my children. I'm so thankful that they are both terrible sleepers, because now I have something to compare myself to. I am not the mother I was when I had my first, although I have so much further to go. God has done an amazing work!

(It's mama Baylee from the future. In just a few short weeks, your baby will start sleeping like a dream. He's now four years old, and I've never met a kid who loves his sleep more. You won't even remember this sleepless stage with him. Hang on, mama!)

But let patience have *its* perfect work, that you may be perfect and complete, lacking nothing. (James 1:4)

PRAYER

Lord, I know I will never be perfect and complete until I see Your face, but I praise God for the struggles that bring me one step closer! Jesus, You are good! Let me remember this truth every minute of the day!

....

....

....

....

....

....

....

continue your personal prayer

POWER TO OVERCOME

Mom guilt is such a hard thing to navigate. As I look back on Brim's two years of life, I feel so guilty. I struggled with postpartum depression the first ten to eleven months of his life, and I felt like I couldn't enjoy it even though I wanted to. I felt so ashamed and so weak that I didn't tell anyone about my struggles. "I'm a Christian mom of a healthy baby boy. I shouldn't be struggling. I should be rejoicing." Yet everything had a dark cloud over it—every giggle, every cute stage, every milestone. As I look at pictures of that time, the memories and the guilt rush in. How could I not enjoy his little life? Why couldn't I just have been stronger? This time, with Conway, I felt like I was doing so much better—loving life, enjoying baby snuggles, and watching my boys grow and love each other. Recently, I started struggling again, and the guilt quickly took over. "I have two beautiful, healthy, happy boys. There's no reason I should be struggling."

I've never thought depression was a real thing; it was just an issue with selfishness that we had the power to overcome ourselves if we simply changed our mindset.

While it may be true that depression is in some ways an issue with selfishness, I have come to realize in an even stronger way that I don't have the power in myself to do anything. I am weak. I can't pull myself up by my bootstraps. When I try, I fail. When I fail, I fall deeper into self-loathing. I am weak, but I'm in luck, for my God's power is made perfect in weakness!

This time, when I started struggling, I told someone, a couple someones. It helps to get our struggles out in the open and to hear "You're not alone." To have people pray for us and with us! The enemy likes when we hide, feel shame, and try in our prideful way to deal with our struggles ourselves, but it is only when we give our struggles over to Lord and allow other people through the Holy Spirit to speak truth into our lives that we can be healed!

> Therefore confess your sins to each other and pray for each other so that you may be healed. The prayer of a righteous person is powerful and effective. (James 5:16)

PRAYER

Lord, let me be quick to confess my sin. Let me be quick to repent. Let me be quick to seek out Your healing.

....

....

....

....

....

....

....

continue your personal prayer

GOOD SOIL
OR WEEDS

There is so much urgency in the scriptures to share the Gospel. Yet I feel as though the tactic of Satan toward Americans especially is to convince us to be very passive, to be distracted by the cares of this life. With all the things happening in our country, I wonder if it isn't an act of grace from God to wake us up. I know I have definitely been more focused on Jesus and the things that truly matter, because of the chaos that has ensued. If all freedom and everything else is taken away, if He is the only one we have, then we will realize He is all we need.

> Therefore hear the parable of the sower: When anyone hears the word of the kingdom, and does not understand *it,* then the wicked *one* comes and snatches away what was sown in his heart. This is he who received seed by the wayside. But he who received the seed on stony places, this is he who hears the word and immediately receives it with joy; yet he has no root in himself, but endures only for a while. For when tribulation or persecution arises because of the word, immediately he stumbles. Now he who received seed among the thorns is he who hears the word, and the cares of this world and the deceitfulness of riches choke the word, and he becomes unfruitful. But he who received seed on the good ground is he who hears the word and understands *it,* who indeed

bears fruit and produces: some a hundredfold, some sixty, some thirty. (Matthew 13:18–23)

One question I've been pondering for a few weeks now is, what kind of seed am I? I do not want to be a lukewarm Christian. I do not want to live this life focused on the cares of the world. I want to be a seed producing fruit in abundance. In order to do this, my heart needs to be soft soil. It needs to be nourished and watered with the water of the Word.

PRAYER

Lord, let my heart be the good soil. Use my life to produce abundant fruit!

....

....

....

....

....

....

....

....

....

continue your personal prayer

A LITTLE CATCH-UP

This book is meant to be used as a devotional, but it's also sort of my journal. It's me expressing the truths I've been learning along this journey we call life. Well, there were quite a few years in between the last chapter and the next one. You see, I stopped using the gift God gave me of writing for a few years. In this time, I was believing a lie that I had lost the ability, maybe even that God had taken away the gift. That simply wasn't true. I just never put in the time or energy to use the gift.

What's your gift, dear reader? You definitely have one, so don't let the enemy, or anyone else, tell you otherwise. It's very important to your spiritual health that you figure out your specific gifts and that you use them! God has equipped you, right where you are, to be used in a way that only you can. "And who knows but that you have come to your position for such a time as this?" (Esther 4:14 paraphrased).

I thought I would link a bridge between the previous and following chapters. We moved from Texas to Wyoming with a brief three-month stop in Arizona, and we had another baby. So much growth took place not only in our family size and our children's ages but also in our hearts and spiritual lives. I wish it was all recorded, but make no mistake. Jesus is always at work in our hearts.

PRAYER

Lord, reveal to me my spiritual gifts. Let me use those gifts for Your purpose in the sphere of influence, big or small, that You have placed me in. Be glorified in my life.

LORD, I'M AT THE END OF MYSELF

Lord, I'm at the end of myself.

This week, we caught our seventh sickness of the year, and it is a doozy. Our oldest son ended up in the emergency room with major breathing problems, and we thought our baby was headed that way at one point too. While holding my coughing child in the middle of the night, I was asking the Lord, "Why are we going through this? Why are we so sick so often?" And I was reminded of this prayer/poem I wrote:

> Lord, I'm at the end of myself. What a great place to be.
>
> Help me have joy in complete reliance on Thee.
>
> Take my selfishness. Make it faithfulness.
>
> Take my comparison; let me be covered in forgiveness.
>
> You. You are all that can fulfill. All of life is empty without You.
>
> Every day, I wake up with a choice to make. When I choose to eat my daily bread, instead of the world's demands, I find my soul at rest in peace, knowing You're in control.
>
> You. You're all that can fulfill. All of life is empty without You.
>
> So give me peace, give me joy.

Give me all that I can have to bring glory to You,
Lord. Give me trials if that means I'll be more like
you. no matter what life brings.
Because You. You fulfill.

What a sweet moment to be reminded that life's trials, if we let
them, bring us closer to being like Jesus. I've got so far to go, but the
Lord revealed just how far He's brought me, and not one of those
steps in growth have come without trials being the vehicle for change
in my heart.

Consider it pure joy my brothers when ever you face
trials of any kind, because you know that the testing
of your faith produces patience, let patience have
its perfect work so that we might be mature and
complete lacking nothing. (James 1:2–4)

There are people going through much bigger trials than mine.
If that's you, I hope this meets you with so much comfort and
encouragement.

PRAYER

Lord, let me remember You fulfill. You're the purpose for it all.

....

....

....

....

continue your personal prayer

DROWN ME IN YOUR LOVE

Let these words of truth wash over you today. May your day be richly blessed, and may you be refreshed by the sweet love of our Jesus.

Why is it so easy to forget it's all about You, Lord?

When the cares of the world feel like tidal waves, let me drown in Your love instead.

Help me to remember You hold it all together. You're big enough to face my fears. You are never afraid.

Why do I keep forgetting it's all about You, Lord?

When joy feels out of reach, but the reason is a mystery. When time just won't slow down, I feel it slipping away. The kids are growing, but I'm still messing up every day.

Let me sit in Your presence, quiet my mind, take my cares away. Even for a moment, show me Your indescribable peace and let me know you deeper …

You created me. You love me. You are jealous for me. Life is so much sweeter when I take the time to remember that this life is all about You, Lord.

> He is before all things and in Him all things hold together. (Colossians 1:17)

PRAYER

Lord, let me be immersed, saturated, dripping in Your love. Your love changes things. Your love changes me. Let my heart be overflowing.

....

....

....

....

....

....

....

....

....

....

....

....

continue your personal prayer

HOPE AND PEACE

When I fill myself with your promises, how multiplied is my hope and peace. You surround me. Like the chariot armies of angels, You are on my side.

There is no rest like Your rest, no peace like Your peace. Thank You for all You do. Thank You for Your provision, even when I'm not paying attention.

Like a loving parent, You provide all our needs. There is no lack in You.

No matter how out of control this life gets, we have You holding on to us. That alone gives me ease in my soul.

Though there is much that causes fear, who is stronger than You, oh Lord?

So watch over my kids growing in this world. Protect them. Help me to have wisdom in raising warriors who know the author of it all.

Watch over my marriage, though the enemy seeks to pull it apart. You are the glue that holds us together. When we're close to You, we're close together.

We know how it ends. You win. Thank You for letting me be on your side. Though I have nothing to offer, You still call me Yours.

> But he said to me, "My grace is sufficient for you, for my power is made perfect in weakness." Therefore I will boast all the more gladly of my weaknesses, so that the power of Christ may rest upon me. (2 Corinthians 12:9)

PRAYER

Lord, You are hope. You are peace. When I have You, I have everything I need. Let my heart feel this deeply.

....

....

....

....

....

....

....

....

....

....

....

....

....

continue your personal prayer

HOW BLESSED

Waking up to a glorious morning. How blessed I am to be alive. Your love is sweet. Your grace is sufficient.

Let me be focused on You today. Let me glory in Your unfailing faithfulness. Let me count every blessing throughout the day, for it is a blessing just to live in Your presence.

Change my perspective. When challenges arise, let me see the beauty in every inconvenience. For even the inconvenient has a purpose. Be my strength. Be my self-control.

Let patience feel attainable, though it's the last thing I want to pray for. Let me be quick to repent when I fail.

Let today be the only day in view, for this moment is the only one I'm promised.

> Blessed is the one
> who does not walk in step with the wicked
> or stand in the way that sinners take
> or sit in the company of mockers,
> but whose delight is in the law of the Lord,
> and who meditates on his law day and night.
> (Psalm 1:1–2)

PRAYER

Lord, let praise be always on my lips. Let my heart sing of thankfulness all the day long.

WHAT IT MEANS

When I truly contemplate what it means to be Yours, I can't help but rejoice.

Me, the girl who was headed for destruction—you love me! So humbling it is to be called clean. I know me better than any person, but You know me deeper still. You know me fully, yet You love me unconditionally. There is nothing I can do to escape Your love.

Let Your love be at the forefront of my mind today, because then and only then can I remember to live wholeheartedly for You—to let Your spirit live through me, to have your patience with my kids, to love the way You love.

Let me not simply speak it and think it; let me live out Your character. Let Your fruit be evident in my life. You alone satisfy my soul.

There are no words to express my gratitude for Your sacrifice. Thank You is what I'll keep saying till my last breath.

> For I am persuaded, that neither death, nor life, nor angels, nor principalities, nor powers, nor things present, nor things to come, Nor height, nor depth, nor any other creature, shall be able to separate us from the love of God, which is in Christ Jesus our Lord. (Romans 8:38–39)

PRAYER

Thank You that Your love is secure. Thank You that I don't have to wonder. Thank You for being unconditional.

FAITHFUL

L ord, You are so good. Help me to rest in Your faithfulness. Take my sins and wash them away! Why am I so restless? Why does my anxiety overwhelm me sometimes? Don't I know who hung the stars? I should be the most at ease because You watch over me.

So bring peace to my weary soul. Let the chaos and noise be quieted. Hold me close to Your heart so all I hear is Your still, small voice.

> You, God, are my God,
> Earnestly I seek you;
> I thirst for you,
> My whole being longs for you,
> In a dry and parched land where there is no water.
> I have seen you in the sanctuary, and beheld your power and your glory.
> Because your love is better than life, my lips will glorify you. (Psalm 63:1–3)

BE MY GOD.

Do I believe in Your power? Do I believe You are Lord over it all? Sometimes I feel so powerless, and I am, but I fail to rely on You, for in You, strength is found.

Often, I call You, Lord. I say that I trust in You, but maybe I don't even realize sometimes I'm far from You. At times, I pray, but I don't really feel You; my mind is so distracted. I have to ask my own heart, "Do you believe? Because you're acting like you're your own strength." My heart and soul are not the problem. For they have seen enough and felt enough to know that You are my God, my Lord, my Savior, my redeemer, my friend. It's my mind that's hard to tame; my mind keeps thinking I can do it myself. I can't.

So be God of my mind. Take control of my thoughts. Quiet the chaos and let me focus on You. I do believe, but help the unbelief that creeps in all too easily. Help me convince the parts of my mind that wage war against my spirit. And let what I know to be true reflect in my actions today.

> For in my inner being I delight in Gods law; but I see another law at work in me, waging war against the law of my mind and making me a prisoner of the law of sin at work within me. (Romans 7:22–23)

PRAYER

Lord, please let all of this be true of my life in this moment.

....

....

....

....

....

....

....

continue your personal prayer

NO MATTER WHAT COMES

Lord, you are good!

No matter what comes, you are good!

Though it's hard to see in the moment, You have purpose in it all.

Thank you for your goodness, thank you for your order!

Help me to always trust you, for there is no other way to have true joy.

When I sit and contemplate your goodness, there my soul finds rest and my spirit is at peace.

You already are the author, so Lord be editor of my life.

Take anything out that doesn't bring glory to your name.

Bring conviction back anywhere that I've become numb, if I have ignored your still small voice, let me hear it once again.

I know I'm under construction, but how much harder it must be to construct a self-sabotaging project. Let me be planted and unmoved, on a firm foundation so that the construction can take place.

Let me live wholeheartedly for you.

> You will say to me then, "Why does He still find fault? For who has resisted His will?" But indeed, O man, who are you to reply against God? Will the thing formed say to him who formed *it*, "Why have you made me like this?" Does not the potter have power over the clay, from the same lump to make one vessel for honor and another for dishonor?
> —Romans 9:19–24

What if God, wanting to show His wrath and to make His power known, endured with much long-suffering the vessels of wrath prepared for destruction, that He might make known the riches of His glory on the vessels of mercy, which He had prepared beforehand for glory, even we, who He called, not of the Jews only but also of the Gentiles?

PRAYER

Lord, You are sovereign. Your ways are higher. You see it all. Your plans are better. I trust You even when I don't understand.

....

....

....

....

....

....

....

....

....

....

continue your personal prayer

THIS ONE IS FOR THE PARENTS AND FUTURE PARENTS

I know there is so much pain around this subject in the realm of infertility. I'm not trying to rub salt in that wound. My heart hurts for the many people facing this issue, but parenthood is of far more importance than our world ascribes to it.

I would argue that raising kids is the *most* important job we will ever have in our lives. Whether you're a Christian or not, that statement is true. You're raising the next generation. You are leaving a legacy. Whether that's a good legacy or a bad one is up to you, but if you're a parent, you are already leaving one.

That obligation doesn't pause because we have our own aspirations. Recently, I had to take inventory of my endeavors. I realized I was far more concerned with my own selfish ambitions than raising my kids. They were existing in my life rather than me laying down my desires for them.

I'm not even saying that anything I do outside of being a mama is inherently bad. There are moms who do it very well. I'm not one of those moms. Anytime I tried to do the things that were easily interrupted by my little ones' needs, I'd find myself easily irritated, impatient, and trying to push them off to do something else so they didn't bother me. There have been plenty of voices I've paid far too much attention to, ones that have said, "It's good. You're doing what you need to do. You're making money. You're showing your kids a good example of a hard worker." But I knew that was wrong when I was so stressed all the time that I was not showing them kindness or grace. I'm wasting what is a very short season of shaping and training them, and worst of all, I'm not showing them the love of Jesus with my short temper due to the stress I've piled on.

I've come to realize that now is not the time to chase what I'm chasing. Now is the time to train up my children, and I guarantee I will not regret it in the future. I will not regret laying down the stress I've been carrying, trying to be it all. To be a happy mama who has time to go catch bugs with my boys or play endless amounts of airplane mechanic … they are only young once. This is not to add to the mom guilt we all already face. It's to hopefully encourage moms who think of themselves as "just moms" to realize they need to be *nothing* more than that! No matter how much the world wants to downplay that job, there is nothing more important than taking it seriously.

> Raise up a child in the way he should go, and when
> he is old he will not depart from it. (Proverbs 22:6)

PRAYER

Please help me live selflessly when it comes to parenting. Let me live in service to my family as unto You.

....

....

....

....

....

continue your personal prayer

WHEN THE ATTACKS
ARE WITHIN

When the attacks are within …

One thing I have come to know for sure in my walk with Jesus is if you're doing anything for Jesus, you're going to be attacked.

Most of my attacks are from within. For a lot of years now, I've struggled hard with insecurity, feeling inadequate and inferior. I've always played this sin off in my mind as "being humble." After all, I am inadequate, the Bible teaches us that "we fall short of the glory of God" (Romans 3:23). What's the difference between being humble and walking in the sin of insecurity? Well, one is a virtue, and one is debilitating me from living out my purpose in the Lord. I have been given spiritual gifts in the Lord, and so have you. Writing is one of mine, and I'm not using the gifts I've been given because I tell myself, "I'm not qualified." This is sin. I'm not qualified. I'm not talented in and of myself. That is why God can be glorified through someone like me! That is what I will choose to boast in. God can use even me, so He most definitely can use you too! Don't let Satan debilitate you, and definitely don't let him disguise it as being virtuous. Be obedient and let Jesus use your life!

PRAYER

Lord, protect my heart and help me be obedient.

MOTHERHOOD

There is no greater blessing than to be a mother. When I became a mom five years ago, I was the most selfish person. I could go on for hours about all the struggles I had with motherhood those first couple years, but I won't do that to you. I never would have known about this illness of selfishness had I not had my precious babies. I was used to sleeping when I wanted, going wherever I wanted, whenever I wanted, and eating whatever I wanted without it affecting anyone else (breastfeeding moms, if you know, you know). I struggled so much more in that first year with my loss of freedom than I ever expected. I was self-centered to the core.

I now have three kids, five years old and under. Let me tell you how amazed I am by the faithfulness of Jesus to change me! I am a *far* cry from a perfect mom, but when I tell you the work of Jesus in my life is incredible, I say this in the humblest way. It would blow your mind. I think about that new, overwhelmed, anxiety-ridden mother that I was, and I don't even recognize her. I prayed hard that the Lord would change me, and although it was a much, much slower process than I would have liked, He has been so incredibly faithful to do just that! I've got a long way to go, but I just wanted to offer some encouragement! If you're in a stage right now where you feel like you will always struggle in this particular area, I'm here to tell you to keep up the fight! And for some serious encouragement, think back to a struggle you used to have that you never thought you'd be free from! Are you free? This too shall pass! In a year, or two, or five! You'll look back and think, *That's incredible. That struggle is nothing now.*

Be on your guard, stand firm in the faith, be courageous and strong, do everything in love. (1 Corinthians 16:13–14)

PRAYER

Lord, thank You for Your continuous work in my life. Thank You for the encouraging moments of being reminded where I was and how far You've brought me. It gives me so much hope for the future.

....

....

....

....

....

....

....

....

....

....

continue your personal prayer

MUCH BETTER THAN
A ROM-COM

Our culture is obsessed with romance movies.

It's easy to see why. Everyone has this desire to be loved deeply, to have a passionate love that never gives up, to have someone commit to you even when they know your faults, your mess. Everyone wants a sacrificial love that chooses us no matter what. Someone who'll send one letter a day for a year to get us back, or read to us when we're old and can't remember who they are. Someone who'll die from hypothermia in frozen water, holding our hand so that we can survive on a floating door, even though it's clearly big enough for two ... but that's beside the point. (If you haven't seen *The Notebook* or *The Titanic* movies, I'm not recommending them, but these examples will not make sense to you).

We all know a romantic story or two, and they're all sappy and corny and sometimes cause irritation because it not real life.

But the reality is none of those stories of sacrificial love can even hold a candle to Gods' love story He wrote to us. Those rom-coms are not realistic because people are imperfect and incapable of absolute sacrificial love all the time. Although we can get a taste of this love with a really great spouse, we are still incapable of this kind of love in every moment.

We desire this type of unending, unconditional love because we were made to have this kind of relationship with Jesus. He wrote the ultimate love story by choosing us time and again, dying on the cross for that relationship to even be possible, for the slight chance that you might choose Him. Though we are so imperfect, He loves us perfectly. If you haven't met Him yet, I can't recommend Him enough!

> For God so loved the world, that he gave his only begotten Son, that whosoever believeth in him should not perish, but have everlasting life. (John 3:16)

> That if you confess with your mouth the Lord Jesus and believe in your heart that God has raised Him from the dead, you will be saved. For with the heart one believes unto righteousness, and with the mouth confession is made unto salvation. (Romans 10:9–10)

PRAYER

Lord, thank You for Your unconditional love. Let me love You with all of my heart! Let me be completely sold out for You.

....

....

....

....

....

....

....

continue your personal prayer

LOVE, ACCEPTANCE, AND URGENCY

We all have that thing deep inside, that thing we think, *If they knew this, they'd reject me.*

Nothing is hidden from Jesus. He sees every broken part of us, and yet He loves us perfectly.

If you don't know Jesus, well, you probably hate this book … but I'm proud of you for sticking with it. Let me give you just a few simple reasons why you should choose a relationship with Jesus.

None of us like talking about death, but Jesus talked more about hell than He talked about heaven. Why? Because hell is a very real place. Jesus died. Jesus paid the price—your price, my price—as a free gift of salvation so that *no one* would go to hell. He holds this gift out to you, but you must accept it to have it be yours. The same way that if I gave you a gift, you would have to take it from my hands for you to own it. It really is that easy.

But the urgency part of this message is this: you don't know how long you've got left on this earth. If you die apart from a relationship with Him, without accepting that free gift, you will spend eternity apart from Him, in hell. At that point, your, possibly undecided, decision is made. Let today be the day of salvation. Don't put it off. You do not know for sure if you have that option.

Apart from where you'll spend eternity, as important as that is, if you're living apart from Him, you probably feel like you're missing something in life. There's a hopelessly sad feeling of "Is this really it?" The answer to that question and the reason for that feeling is that we were created to be in relationship with Jesus. You haven't yet met your purpose for existing if you don't know the one you were created to know.

Let today be the day of salvation.

The other side of that urgency message goes out to the ones who do know Jesus. Share Him!

I was so convicted this week for staying in my safe little comfort zone. I'm sitting back and letting people live in hopelessness and die in sin when I know the cure! Jesus! I hope that convicts you to action!

Second Peter 3:4 says, "They will say, 'Where is the promise of his coming? For ever since the fathers fell asleep, all things are continuing as they were from the beginning of creation.'"

This way of thinking has entered the church and has caused complacency. Jesus *is* coming back! People do need to hear about Him!

PRAYER

Lord, I pray for revival in this nation. I pray for Your people to wake up and take Your call to action, to tell a dying world of Your truth!

....

....

....

....

....

....

....

continue your personal prayer

DAVID

David's story gave me so much hope.

David, a man after God's own heart (1 Samuel 13:14, Acts 13:22), found himself in a dark place. He had committed adultery with a close friend's wife and then murdered his friend to cover up his sins. To be seen as righteous, he then married his murdered friend's wife. Being humbled at the end of all of this, he repented and found forgiveness.

As a pastor's daughter, I was very rebellious to my parents. At twelve years old, I was always in trouble. On one such occasion, I found myself in my room, waiting for my dad to deliver the terms of my grounding sentence. He asked me a very simple yet profound question. "Baylee, do you think you really know Jesus personally?"

"No," I replied bluntly, knowing the answer emphatically.

"Do you want to?" he asked so gently.

"Yes," I said with earnest. And in that moment, the weight of the world was lifted from my shoulders.

Later in the day, my mom got a call from my friend's mom saying that her daughter had ratted me out for sneaking out of the house in the middle of the night (something we had done many times together). When my mom asked me if this was true, I did what I had done so many other times before. I lied. But this time was different. I instantly got sick to my stomach. I had convictions I had never had before. Such a sweet, tangible sign of the inward change God had just done in my life. I had to come clean.

Fast-forward seven years. I'm nineteen. I find myself in an extremely unhealthy relationship. I'm broken beyond what I believe I can bear. I'm ready to die. I believe that I've blown it too badly to be forgiven by my family, let alone God. After all, I'm a Christian, yet I'm living in sin. How could Jesus ever forgive me? How could I ever turn around and face Him?

David, called a man after God's heart, did incredible things through the power of God early in his life. He finds himself in major sin. He repented and was forgiven, restored in right relationship with the Lord.

We are *never* too far gone! I have experienced the power of the forgiveness and restoration of the Lord personally! He is the healer of *all* broken things! *Never* let Satan lie to you! You can turn around in any mess! He is happy to have you back in His arms! If you're caught in sin, turn around. He's right there waiting for you.

PRAYER

Thank You for being the incredibly forgiving and merciful God that You are! Thank You that no matter what mess I'm in, You're always ready to forgive me.

....

....

....

....

....

....

....

continue your personal prayer

PRIDE

I fear pride in my life. Pride is a sneaky thing. It's so incredibly easy to fall into and so hard to recognize in ourselves. I can get prideful over anything! Someone comes up and tells me, "You are so humble," and in that instant, if I'm not careful, I could be prideful about being humble. Knowing I'm so susceptible to pride, I've found myself praying more than ever that the Lord will help me recognize pride in my life and help me eradicate it so that I can be humble and kind.

> Pride comes before destruction and a haughty spirit before a fall. (Proverbs 16:18)

Pride can rear its ugly head in many different forms—gossip or slandering, judging the struggles of others, comparisons, believing that I'm better than someone else spiritually, physically, in my work ethic, and so on. It can be seen in an attitude of anger or entitlement, the belief that I deserve something.

I deserve death. I deserve hell. I deserve separation for eternity from God. I have nothing to judge in others when I remember I have been so forgiven myself. Thank You, Jesus. You don't give me what I deserve!

I've been taking inventory in my life of the ways I tend to be prideful. Sometimes it's by the moment that I have to remind myself of the cross and the blood that was shed for me, and I'd challenge you to do the same.

PRAYER

Lord, purify my heart! Clean out my heart and eradicate pride from my life. Let my love for others be pure.

....

....

....

....

....

....

....

....

....

....

....

....

continue your personal prayer

AWE

In awe of Him.

You are the creator of the universe, the creator of the stars, galaxies, and the mountains so big they're overwhelming. You created snowflakes and tear ducts. Our bodies are so intricately made to work together. You designed our bodies to heal themselves. You designed our souls to worship You.

You, author of it all, met here with me this morning. You love me. I can't even wrap my mind around that fully. You already know me. You pursue me. You want me to know You, to learn Your character deeply. You don't want me to just read a book about You (not that the Bible is just a book, but sometimes I think we read it as such) and move on with my day. You want me to talk with You, to meet with You, to experience Your goodness, to love You!

I was thinking about it in this way today. What if Chad woke up in the morning and didn't say a word to me? If he just sat down and read my writings for the day, closed it, and left for work. I would be saying, "Um, hello? That's not a relationship with me. You just read a few thoughts I had. I'm right here."

But sometimes that's exactly what I do with the Lord. I'll read or listen to His Word but not actually talk with or commune with Him. He's sitting there, and I just pick up His book to read without so much as a hi. I know this is kind of a funny way to look at it, but it's true! He desires a relationship with us, not just an "I read" check of the box on the list.

And this is eternal life, that they know you, the only true God, and Jesus Christ whom you have sent. (John 17:3 ESV)

For the word of God is quick, and powerful, and sharper than any twoedged sword, piercing even to the dividing asunder of soul and spirit, and of the joints and marrow, and is a discerner of the thoughts and intents of the heart. (Hebrews 4:12)

PRAYER

Lord, let me live in awe of You.

....

....

....

....

....

....

....

....

....

continue your personal prayer

JOB

Reading Job is always a struggle for me. I've read it twice this year, and it's hard to fully understand and to not ask why. Why did a righteous man have to endure so much heartache, ridicule, and suffering?

While reading it this time around, I was thinking about his "friends" and what they had to say. I noticed their doctrine is very messed up; they believe that evil comes upon us because of what we do in life. While correction does come through the seeds of sin we plant, evil is not of God; nor does evil come upon us as a punishment for doing wrong. I believe a lot of us could fall into this line of doctrine as well, maybe without even fully realizing it. Of course we know, because of the book of Job, this isn't the case. Job was not being punished; he was being tested. It's easy for me to look at this account and think, *God is being so cruel to Job.* Do you know what would be more cruel? For God not to test him. What is this life if it's the only good we'll ever have? If we just have riches and blessings here, but then we die and spend eternity apart from Jesus, what good would that do for us? This life, even if we live one hundred years, is but a vapor. Trying to hold onto it is like trying to grasp water; it's slipping away. Nobody wants to be tested, but we should welcome it. "For the testing of our faith develops perseverance. Let perseverance finish its work so that we may be mature and complete lacking nothing" (James 1:3–4). I would rather be tested in this life and find that my faith is true than die and realize that Jesus never knew me (Matthew 7:22–29).

I believe the book of Job is the only source we need to refute the prosperity gospel or the name-it-and-claim-it, manifestation gospel.

"In this life we will have trouble, but take heart for He has overcome the world" (John 16:33).

I know a lot of people are dealing with some hard stuff right now. I pray that, like Job, you hold on to your faith and never let go of Jesus. He really is the only anchor we've got in this life. Hold tight, my friends!

PRAYER

Lord, let me see Your mercy in every circumstance. You are good even when things don't make sense.

....

....

....

....

....

....

....

....

....

....

continue your personal prayer

ESCAPE THE CITY!

Last night, I went down a rabbit trail of thoughts. There was once a time I was living a very hypocritical life, saying one thing but living and doing something else ...

When I started thinking about all the people who knew my life of blatant sin and also knew what I was saying, the truth of the Gospel I know to be true, I felt guilty for the witness I had ruined. I had added to those people's excuses for why they don't need to be a Christian. After all, I knew the truth but was clearly living contrary to it.

Reading the story of Lot this morning, I think he was in a similar compromising situation. When the angels came into the city, he instantly acted as a child who didn't want his parents to see the mess he made in the other room. He said, "Turn into my house. Don't go into the city." He knew he was living in an immoral place. There is more to the story that shows us the major evil he had come to accept as normal in his life. But I'm not going to get into that right now. (I encourage you to read it in Genesis 19.)

When the angels told him to get out of the city, it says he went to the house of his sons-in-laws, and they didn't believe him.

"Get out of here, for destruction is coming."

"How would you know? You think you know the truth? You think you talk to angels? You must be joking. You live the same way as us."

This is similar to how the world will react to us if we allow ourselves to get comfortable in sin. We all sin, but we cannot get comfortable in it; we must be quick to recognize sin and repent. Sin will always push us away from the Lord and make His voice hard to hear. We must be quick to return to Him.

It goes on to say the angels told Lot to "get out quick because destruction is coming." And it says that he lingered; he had friends there, a livelihood, fun. He was comfortable there.

If we love this life, we'll lose it (John 12:25). Is there a place in your life that you need to flee? Somewhere you need to escape? It's imperative that you run. Don't look back!

When I was thinking last night about living in that life of compromise, I could not be more thankful for God rescuing me from it.

Later in Hebrews 11, Lot is called righteous. Let that encourage us! Lot is called righteous because he simply believed. God can still use our life and our story even after we've messed up. But we must first "escape the city."

PRAYER

Lord, give me strength and courage to escape the city! Let me live wholeheartedly for You.

....

....

....

....

....

....

....

continue your personal prayer

CONCLUSION

If you've stuck through this book to the end, please know I am so honored to have walked this journey with you. I am praying for everyone who is reading this. I'm praying that God will use these words like only He can, to speak to you! If anything spoke to your heart in this book, all glory should be given to God! I pray you will be blessed in your walk with Jesus!

ABOUT THE AUTHOR

Baylee Hefley and her husband have been married seven years. They have three children, with another one on the way. Although very imperfect, they have strived to be devoted to and live by the Word of God in their lives and marriage. They love to see others thrive in their relationship with Jesus as well.

Printed in the United States
by Baker & Taylor Publisher Services